TRISTIA

Books by L. R. Lind

Medieval Latin Studies: Their Nature and Possibilities   1941

The Vita Sancti Malchi of Reginald of Canterbury: A Critical Edition   1942

The Epitome of Andreas Vesalius   1949

Lyric Poetry of the Italian Renaissance: An Anthology with Verse Translations   1954

Ten Greek Plays in Contemporary Translations   1957

Latin Poetry in Verse Translation   1957

Ecclesiale by Alexander of Villa Dei   1958

Berengario da Carpi: A Short Introduction to Anatomy   1959

Vergil's Aeneid   1963

Aldrovandi on Chickens: The Ornithology of Ulisse Aldrovandi   1963

Epitaph for Poets and Other Poems   1966

Problemata Varia Anatomica   1968

Twentieth Century Italian Poetry: A Bilingual Anthology   1974

Johann Wolfgang von Goethe, Roman Elegies and Venetian Epigrams   1974

Studies in Pre-Vesalian Anatomy: Biography, Translations, Documents   1974

OVID: TRISTIA

TRANSLATED BY L. R. LIND

UNIVERSITY OF GEORGIA PRESS
ATHENS

The University of Georgia Press, Athens 30602

Library of Congress Catalog Card Number: 73–88363
International Standard Book Number: 0–8203–0330–5

Printed in the United States of America

To

ARTHUR GORDON RIPPEY

friend and book collector

CONTENTS

INTRODUCTION

The exile of Ovid is one of the most astonishing events in the history of classical Latin literature. The last survivor among the great Augustan poets and the most brilliant and widely read at the time, popular both among fellow writers and in high Roman society, he was suddenly ordered by the emperor Augustus to leave Rome and to dwell indefinitely at Tomis in Moesia on the western coast of the Black Sea. The region is called Dobrudja and lies about sixty-five miles southwest of the closest mouth of the Danube river on the site of the modern Constantza, Rumania. The bleak and chilly climate; the barbarous inhabitants composed of Getes, Sarmatians, Bessi, Ciziges, and other tribes who continually threatened the border town of Tomis and the adjacent area with plunder and warfare; the complete lack of books and of people cultured enough to understand him and his poetry made Ovid's life a continual hell on earth. From A.D. 8, the date of his banishment, until his death sometime after the latest date which can be absolutely confirmed from his poems, the consulship of Graecinus in A.D. 16, Ovid remained at Tomis. While there he wrote his last poems, the *Tristia, Epistulae ex Ponto, Halieutica,* and *Ibis*.

Many conjectures, hypotheses, and mere wild guesses have been advanced to explain the reasons for Ovid's exile. These are collected and evaluated most conveniently in an admirable book by John C. Thibault, *The Mystery of Ovid's Exile* (Berkeley and Los Angeles: University of California Press, 1964). They range throughout a wide variety, all arising from the two most significant words Ovid himself uses in his *Tristia* and *Epistulae ex Ponto* when he refers to the sources of his disgrace: *carmen et error* (*Tristia* II, 207).

The *carmen* is his *Art of Love*, which he mentions frequently as one cause for his downfall. This satirical, mocking parody of didactic verse has been described by many later commentators and scholars as undermining Augustus' program of moral reform and encouraging adultery among the Roman upper classes. But Ovid vigorously and effectively defends himself against this charge, nowhere more ably than in *Tristia* II, the longest elegy of the entire collection (578 lines) and contained in a separate book. It is devoted to a carefully composed oration which reveals Ovid's early training both in rhetoric and law, arranged carefully in accordance with the traditional outline of a law court defense: *exordium* (1–26), *propositio* (27–28), *tractatio* (29–578); the latter falls into two divisions, each ending with an epilogue: *probatio* (29–154) and *epilogus* (155–206), and *refutatio* (207–572) plus *epilogus* (573–578). While the *Art of Love* can be regarded when taken with the other love poems, *Amores and Heroides* (all written before he was forty, after which he turned to the *Metamorphoses*, unfinished at the time of his exile) as damaging evidence of Ovid's elastic morals he points out convincingly that many other well-accepted poets wrote even more lascivious verses than his own—and none of them had been deported for his poems.

The *error* of Ovid's frequent references is much more fertile and ambiguous in the number of hypotheses it has brought forth from the Middle Ages to our own time. They include the following, presented without regard to their relative importance or priority, all of them impossible of proof. Ovid had unwillingly witnessed one of the homosexual acts of the emperor, known throughout his lifetime for his amorous exploits with both sexes as well as for his seduction of his courtiers' wives, such as Terentia, the wife of his minister, Maecenas. Ovid had committed adultery with the younger Julia, Augustus' granddaughter, or had been implicated in one of her more shocking escapades. Ovid had been part of a conspiracy by Silanus, the lover of the younger Julia, to place her brother, Agrippa Postumus, upon the throne. Postumus was exiled in A.D. 7 and Julia in A.D. 8, when Ovid also was exiled. Ovid, who was actually an initiate into the mysteries of Eleusis, was accused of revealing and thus profaning them. Or he had, like Clodius in Cicero's day, attended in disguise the mysteries of the Bona Dea, a woman's goddess at Rome in whose worship the empress Livia took a prominent part. In the course of the mysteries or at another occasion Ovid had seen Livia nude in her bath. Ovid had been connected in some way with another conspiracy, that of L. Aemilius Paulus, who had plotted against Augustus. Paulus was the husband of the younger Julia and consul in A.D. 1. Ovid had taken part in the dynastic ambitions of Livia, the emperor's second wife. According to another equally conjectural view, Ovid had refused to propagandize for Augustus, although here again he replied with the protest in *Tristia* II that he had praised Augustus lavishly. Again, he had become a partisan of Germanicus, Tiberius' nephew and the son of Drusus and the younger Antonia. Agrippina, the wife of Germanicus, later accused Tiberius of poisoning Germanicus in A.D. 19. He had ridiculed Varus for losing the battle of the Teutoberg forest in Germany (which actually occurred one year after Ovid's exile, in A.D. 9) and thus incurred the animosity of Augustus.

These, and other equally unconvincing hypotheses, could arise primarily because our information is so scanty and vague that conjecture rushes in to fill the vacuum where facts are absent. We cannot now know the truth of the matter because the two major parties to the exile, Ovid and Augustus, chose deliberately to leave us in the dark. It is clear, however, that Ovid's fault (he never admits to a crime) was not treason, conspiracy, murder, adultery, bribery, or any other crime punishable by Roman courts and that he was sent away from Rome after a harsh personal interview with the emperor and without a trial. The official pretext for his banishment may well have been Ovid's *Art of Love* or his entire corpus of love poetry, which he ceased to write after A.D. 8. We have no contemporary records on the event and especially lack Suetonius' life of Ovid, which surely was contained in his *De Poetis* and which might have given us the details we now lack. The *error* seems to have been something Ovid saw with his own eyes: and with that we must remain content, perhaps forever.

Ovid was "relegated," not banished in the true technical sense; hence he could hope for pardon and set to writing while on the very voyage to Tomis upon a work of self-justification, special pleading, flattery, protest, and logical argument in order to change Augustus' mind—or, failing that, at least to obtain permission to spend his exile in a more agreeable place than Tomis. The results of this determined campaign were the *Tristia*, "Sad Poems," and their later companions, the *Epistulae ex Ponto*, or "Letters from the Pontus." One of the chief differences between these two sets of poems is the fact that in the *Epistulae* he addressed his correspondents by name while in the *Tristia* he suppressed names, except for Perilla, in order not to embarrass the friends whom he had charged with the task of interceding at court for him.

The *Tristia* consist of fifty poems divided into five books (of which Book II consists of one long elegy), a total of 3,573 lines. Although Ovid speaks with tearful scorn of these poems as below his top level of achievement and by their very purpose destined to be all too monotonously devoted to a single frequently recurring theme, they show nonetheless a high standard of rhetorical polish and ingenuity. In particular, they show a keen command of the psychological devices needed to work upon the emperor's better nature. Book II is an especially effective logical argument in which Ovid ceases to play as elsewhere upon whatever sympathy he might have been able to arouse and presents his case like a good defense lawyer. It is possible, furthermore, to interpret many passages of the *Tristia* as well as of the *Epistulae* as in reality veiled innuendoes and covert mockery of the sort which appears frequently elsewhere in Ovid's poems. This is an aspect of his total works which has not been investigated thoroughly in print as yet and which amounts to a rather impressive collection of evidence for Ovid's downright anti-Augustan sentiment. I hope that the first attempts along this line, carried out by a former student of mine, may one day be presented to readers. I have not tried to reflect this preliminary investigation in my translation, where I follow in the main accepted and conventional interpretations, based upon the recent Latin text of the *Tristia* by Georg Luck (Heidelberg: Carl Winter, 1967) which I have translated throughout.

The books of the *Tristia* (with the exception of Book II because of its special semi-legal nature) reveal a fairly consistent pattern. Each of Books I, III, IV, and V contain, first, an address to his book, the *Tristia*, which he sends as his humble ambassador to Rome apparently book by book as these were completed; even II opens with a reproach to his books in general and not the *Tristia* in particular. Then follow in each book, except II, an elegy to a faithful friend (sometimes to more than one); to his wife (Book V has three elegies to her); to an enemy or detractor at Rome; and an epilogue, which in IV becomes instead the famous autobiographical elegy, 10, in which Ovid gives us more information about himself than any Latin writer has done until the Middle Ages. The remaining elegies in these four books are autobiographical also. In I they describe his harrowing journey to Tomis; in III, the sole etiological elegy in the *Tristia*, on the origin of Tomis; his rigorous life there; springtime in the place, and Ovid's birthday there; in IV his obsession with time as it affects him in its passing (he describes himself as old, grey-haired, and decrepit); and in V his life among the barbarians, the evils of Tomis and his thoughts as in his illness he reproaches a friend for not writing—the ancient complaint of exiles. One elegy (V, 5) is devoted to his wife's birthday and another to Perilla, his literary friend and disciple (III, 7).

The *Tristia* have not in modern times at least found a translator to turn them into serviceable English elegiacs except for *Elegies* III, 10 and 12, translated with mellow felicity by Henry Wadsworth Longfellow. The style of the *Tristia* flows with typical Ovidian ease and grace from topic to topic. His favorite devices and figures of speech recur in these poems with a familiar if sometimes a bit tedious repetition. Puns and comparisons, soliloquies and the figure adynaton ("as many as . . ."), prayers, invocations, word-plays (the frequent association of *carmen* and *crimen* may well be one of these), and all of his earlier rhetorical tricks appear again and again.

One must be patient, I feel, with Ovid's repetition not only of devices but of his central appeal: "rescue me, Caesar, or anybody else who can do so, from barbarous Tomis!" After all, this is the purpose of the *Tristia*, and it remains for us to note how really effective are the changes he rings upon his agonizing theme. His sole remaining recourse was his talent for verse, and no one has used it so eloquently, with so much genuine pathos, and with such justifiable pleading in the entire literature of exile. He had committed no crime, had not been convicted in any court. His offense, whatever it was, had been punished with unusual and unjustifiable severity; no poet before him had ever suffered such a fate. Whatever subversion of morals his poetry might have promoted, it could not have been a motivating force or even a significant contributing factor to the actual depravity of Rome's upper classes in the Augustan period. The *Art of Love* is clearly no more than a symptom instead of a sinister encouragement to laxity of morals. The legislation on morality which Augustus instituted was called forth by a situation more serious and deep-seated than the superficial one reflected by Ovid in his playful handbook on lovemaking.

Only one other famous poet in European literary history has suffered exile as Ovid did—and in almost the same region: Alexander Pushkin. He was banished to Kishinev in Moldavia for expressing his views on political liberty under the Russian czars in 1820. Ovid appears in Pushkin's poetry in *Eugene Onegin*, *The Gypsies*, and especially in his *Epistle to Ovid*. Pushkin read the *Tristia* and *Epistulae ex Ponto* of Ovid with great sympathy and understanding, taking a much more balanced view of them as well as of the hypotheses current in his day about the reasons for Ovid's exile. The parallels between his own exile and that of Ovid were keenly apparent to him. He denied Voltaire's assertion that Ovid had been banished for a love affair with the elder Julia, the daughter of Augustus, pointing out the absurdity of such a view. Pushkin admired particularly the nature description in the *Tristia*, and borrowed certain analogous passages for his poem, *The Gypsies*, such as the coupling of *bones* and *host*, *ossa* and *hospita* (*kosti* and *gosti* in Russian, with an obvious pun) from *Tristia* III, 3, 64–65. In fact, Pushkin was one of the first to recognize the essential pathos and humanity of Ovid's poems from exile, and in his own poetry joined hands with the Latin poet across eighteen hundred years.

Our time has witnessed a series of violent social upheavals in Europe and Asia which have produced not only genocide but the wholesale exile of innocent people. America has received many of them and become the better for its hospitality. The entire story of these catastrophic events is told in Paul Tabori's recently published book, *The Anatomy of Exile;* but whatever the details, the history of the exile of the artist begins for the western world with the banishment of certain Greek lyric poets and philosophers and in the Roman world with that of Ovid. It is instructive to read his poetic protests in the *Tristia* and to reflect upon the immense damage which repressive governments and tyrants have managed to inflict upon some of their superior individuals throughout the centuries.

L. R. Lind

Lawrence, Kansas
April 15, 1973

OVID: TRISTIA

BOOK I

1

Little book, I don't begrudge it; you'll go to the City without me,
    Ay, to the place where your master isn't permitted to go!
Off with you, but in disheveled dress as is proper for exiles;
    Unhappy one, wear the clothes that befit my miserable state.
5 Vaccinium dye will not stain with red the sheathe that will hold you—
    That's not the color which suits one who is broken with grief—
Nor minium glow on your title nor cedar oil soak your papyrus,
    Nor will your white roll-end be set off with black horn.
Decorations like these may adorn the books of happy authors:
10   It is becoming for you to remember the sadness that's mine.
Your edges will not be trimmed down and polished with soft stone of pumice,
    In order that you may appear with your hair frayed out in a mess.
Don't be ashamed of erasures; he who will see them will realize
    They were not made by a pen: they are the stains of my tears.

I

15 Go, book, greet with my words the places which are so dear to me:
　　　　I shall set foot there, of course, with the only "foot" that's allowed.
　　If anyone there shall recall me, as happens among common people,
　　　　If there shall be one who asks how I am doing, by chance,
　　Say I'm alive, that's all, but don't say my luck's looking better
20 　　　Nor tell him the fact I'm alive is due to the gift of a god.
　　If those who read you shall ask additional questions, turn silent,
　　　　Beware lest you carelessly tell something you shouldn't reveal!
　　Straightway the reader will bring back my misdeeds to mind when he's prompted,
　　　　And I'll be gossiped about as Public Enemy One.
25 Take care you stick up for me even though insults will sting you;
　　　　Although my case isn't good your defense will bolster it up.
　　Some one you'll find who will sigh for me because I am exiled
　　　　And not be able to read my poems through with dry cheeks;
　　Who'll silently hope in his heart, lest some ill-willed person should hear him,
30 　　　That Caesar, grown softer, might make the exile he ordered less harsh.
　　I too shall pray my well-wisher, whoever he is, shall not suffer,
　　　　He who wishes the gods may be kind to poor devils like me,
　　And whatever he wishes be granted, the emperor's wrath be abated
　　　　And that he permit me to die here in my ancestral home.
35 Book, as you carry out orders, perhaps there'll be those who will blame you
　　　　And you'll be valued below the praise that my talent should bring.
　　It is the judge's duty to rule on both facts and their context;
　　　　If he rules on the latter you'll be entirely safe.
　　Poems that succeed are the product of minds that are happy and peaceful;
40 　　　Clouds lie upon my breast, troubled with sudden dismay.
　　Poetry calls for retreat and quiet times for the writer;
　　　　Me the wild winter, the sea, me the winds toss about.

2

Dread of all sorts spoils a poem; I am distraught and I'm thinking
    A sword is thrust at my throat, now, now about to plunge in.
45   A judge who is fair will marvel as well at what I am doing
    And read my writing, such as it is, with forgiving eyes.
Give me Homer himself and surround him with dire misfortune,
    All of his talent would fail, crushed beneath so many ills.
Remember to travel, my volume, without any longing for glory,
50   Don't be ashamed when they read you not to have pleased them at all.
Dame Fortune presents us an aspect by no means so shining with favor
    That you should begin to count up all of the praise that you're due.
While I was happy-go-lucky I was touched by a love to be famous,
    There was an ardor within me to seek a name for myself;
55   If I hate the poems that destroyed me, although not the zeal to make verses,
    Let this be enough: it was talent that gained me an exile's flight.

But go you, however, in place of me to see Rome (it's permitted).
    Gods above bring it about! I wish I could now be my book.
Don't think because it's as a pilgrim you're going to visit so ample
60   A city as Rome that you're coming completely unknown to its folk.
Although you may lack any title they'll know you at once by your color;
    Although you may wish to conceal it there isn't a doubt that you're mine.
Enter, however, in secret so my other poems may not harm you;
    They're not, as they once were, in favor, enjoying approval by all.
65   If there is someone who reasons because you are mine that you must be
    Unfit to be read and then throws you out of his lap and away,
Tell him: "Look at my title: I'm not any handbook on loving;
    That earlier opus of mine has paid for its sins as deserved."
Perhaps you may think I should send you up into those mansions that tower

3

70 And bid that you climb to the home where Caesar on Palatine dwells.
May those august regions forgive me, the gods who dwell there forgive me!
That citadel flashed out the lightning, sent down the bolt on my head.
I remembered that powers most gentle maintained their abode on that hill top,
But I am afraid of those gods who brought me both sadness and pain.
75 The dove who has felt your claws, you hawk, and was torn by your talons
Now is set flying in fear by the least noise of your wings.
Not far from its fold will wander the lamb, whichever one suffered,
Whose flesh has been rent by the avid teeth of a ravaging wolf.
If Phaethon were still alive he'd avoid the heavens; those horses
80 That once in his folly he longed for, he'd wish not to touch them at all.
I too confess I was fearful of Jupiter's weapons—I'd felt them;
And when he thundered I thought he was hurling his lightning at me.
Whatever Greek sailor has fled from Cape Caphereus, safe with his navy,
Will always thereafter turn sail away from Euboean bays,
85 And my little bark once shaken by storm upon ocean's wide water
Will be loath to approach that place again where once it was struck.

Therefore beware, my book, look timidly round you with caution,
Let it suffice for you to be read by the simple folk.
While Icarus sought on his pinions, too weak, the loftiest region
90 He fell and bestowed his name upon the Icarian Sea.
From here on it's hard to say whether you should use oars or your mainsail;
Both situation and circumstances will give you a plan.
If you are admitted to Caesar in a quiet moment, if every
Condition is right and his anger has blunted its power at last,
95 If there is someone to lead you all frightened and hesitant to him

4

And to speak a few words before him of introduction, approach.
May you arrive on a good day, more fortunate than your own master,
    And reach him there in his palace and lighten my evil lot.
For only as once Achilles did can anyone heal my
100   Wounds; he alone who inflicted them can heal them again.
Take care you don't create havoc there where you wish to be helpful—
    For the hope I hold in my heart is less than the fear I bear—
Don't savage again into action that anger that thus far lay sleeping;
    Beware lest you give him another reason to punish me.
105 When you're received, however, into my innermost study
    And arrive again at your rounded home, my manuscript box,
There you will see ranged in order your brothers, the books I have written,
    All like you from my pen, the fruits of my nocturnal toil.
These are the crowd that will freely present to your sight open titles
110   And easy to read on their backs you'll see everyone with his name.
Three of them hiding in shadow you'll see far off in a corner;
    And thus they teach how to love, something that everyone knows.
Avoid them, or, if you're sufficiently strong of voice to attempt it,
    Scold them and call them "Oedipuses!" Call them "Telegoni!"
115 I warn you, don't love any one of the three if you're fond of your father,
    Don't love any one, I say, even if he teaches you how.
There will also be fifteen volumes about forms that once were transmuted;
    Not long ago these poems were snatched from my very grave.
Tell them, I bid you, to enter among the changed bodies one other:
120   Mine, for my fortune has suffered its own particular change
Since suddenly it has become unlike the fortune I once had,
    One to be wept for now where once on a time it was gay.

If you ask me, indeed I had many other orders to give you,
    But I'm afraid that I'd cause you to be delayed on your road.
125 And if you should carry, book, with you everything I'd have you shoulder
    Too heavy would be the burden you would be destined to bear.
Long is the journey, now hasten! I shall inhabit the farthest
    End of the earth in a country far from my country away.

2

Gods of the sea and the sky—for what except prayer remains to me?—
    Spare me the unbroken planks of my sea-shattered boat,
Do not, I beg, subscribe to the anger of Caesar the Mighty!
    Often one god will assist when some other god crushes you.
5 Mulciber stood against Troia, Apollo defended the city:
    Venus was kind to her Trojans, Pallas was angry toward them.
Saturnian Juno, who favored Turnus, was harsh to Aeneas.
    The latter, however, was safely guarded by Venus' care.
Often fierce Neptune attacked Ulysses, who acted with caution,
10   Often Minerva has snatched him out of her uncle's grasp.
And who will deny me some power, though I do not rate with immortals,
    To stand and protect me too when a god's angry at me?
Wretch that I am, I am wasting words that I speak unavailing.
    While I am speaking the breakers scatter their spray on my lips
15 And terrible Notus, the south wind, is snatching my words nor allows me
    To offer my prayers to the gods nor permits my vows to ascend.
So the very same winds, lest I founder and lose all in only one cause,
    Are blowing away both my sails and my prayers, where nobody knows.

6

Miserable me, what great mountains the waters of ocean are piling!
20   Now, now you would think that they're striking the very stars with their tops.

O what deep valleys the ocean is making where waves are subsiding!
        Now, now you would think they are touching the black depths of Hades itself.
Wherever you look there is nothing except the air and the ocean,
        This one swollen with rollers, that one with menacing clouds.
25   There in between them are howling the winds with their gigantic roaring,
        The waves of the ocean, bewildered, know not which lord to obey.
For now it is Eurus, the east wind, grown strong from its source, the red East;
        Now it is Zephyr set blowing, come late from the distant West.
Now the north wind out of the Arctic comes storming, dry with its coldness,
30   Now south wind that carries its battle directly attacking in front.
The helmsman is caught in dilemma: where shall he flee or go forward?
        His skill as a sailor is useless, bewildered by contrasting fears.

We are lost! There's no doubt of disaster, our hope of salvation has vanished,
        And while I am talking the waters are splashing all over my face.
35   The billows are crushing my spirit, in vain all my prayers to protect me,
        My mouth will receive the wild breakers, they'll overwhelm me at last.
But my loyal wife is weeping for nothing except that I'm exiled:
        Only this evil of mine is she conscious of, this she deplores.
She knows not I'm tossed on an ocean immense, where my body is floating,
40   She knows not the winds are driving nor that my end is at hand.
It is well that I did not allow her to come on board with me also
        Lest, wretch that I am, I should suffer two times the death that is mine.
But now that I perish I know that since she has been spared my misfortune
        I shall survive, I know surely, with half at least of myself.

7

45 Ay me! how swiftly they flash out, the flames from the clouds in the heavens!
How mighty the thunder that rumbles out of the ether's vast vault!
No less lightly the planks of my gunwales are buffetted by the wild waters
Than the heavy catapult's burden shot against walls of a town.
This wave that approaches surpasses all other waves in the ocean:
50 It rushes behind the ninth breaker and precedes the eleventh as well.
I do not fear death, I'm afraid of the miserable form of my dying;
Rescue me out of a shipwreck and death will be only a boon.
It is something of value when man falls by fate or the thrust of a sword blade
To lay down his lifeless body there in the well-known earth
55 And to make last requests of survivors and to hope for a decent interment,
Not to be food for the fishes and lie in a watery grave.
Assume that I'm worthy to perish by such a death: not alone shall
I die; must my fate bear down with it my innocent friends as well?
"By gods above, by the green gods whose dominion lies over the ocean,
60 Put an end now at last to your raging and stop both your threats against me,
And the life that the most gentle anger of Caesar has granted salvation
Allow me to carry off with me to the place where I'm ordered to flee.
If the fate of which I'm deserving you wish that it now should destroy me,
By the judgment of Caesar himself my fault was not worthy of death.
65 If Caesar had now desired to send me to Stygian waters
For this task he would not have required any assistance from you.
He has the power to spill my blood with impunity ample;
That which he has given he's able to take back whenever he likes.
Now you who are crushed, I am certain, by no wicked crime you've committed
70 Be contented at last with the evils that I have brought down on my head.
Nor yet if all of you wished to save a poor miserable human,
A creature who's perished completely cannot be rescued again.

8

Even if seas should subside and winds become favorable to me,
　　Even if you should spare me I'd be an exile still.
75　It's not from a lust for riches piled up without any limit
　　That I plow the wide open sea or to sell my goods for a price,
　My course is not set for Athens to which once as a student I traveled
　　Nor to visit the cities of Asia nor places I've seen once before;
　Not to set my sail for the noble city named for Alexander
80　In order to view your delights, O Nile where the people are gay,
　That I hope for fair winds to blow me—what person could ever believe this?
　　It is the land of Sarmatians to which my rigging is turned.
　I am obliged to make landfall on the wild shores of the 'Unlucky Ocean,'
　　And I lament that my flight from my country so slowly proceeds.
85　To look upon townsfolk of Tomis, I don't know where in the world they are,
　　I'm making my journey a short one, reduced by means of my prayers.
　So if you love me restrain those monstrous great waves of the ocean
　　And let your powers of heaven be kindly to my little boat.
　If, rather, you hate me then guide me forward to the bidden landfall:
90　Part of my punishment lies in the region chosen for me.
　Blow me—what am I doing here?—swift winds in my sail-yards!
　　Why do my sails continue to hug the Italian coast?
　This is not what Caesar ordered: why hold a man he has exiled?
　　Let the land of the Pontic region look at last on my face.
95　He orders it and I deserved it: against charges he laid upon me
　　I think it neither right nor respectful to defend myself legally.
　However, if acts done by mortals deceive never gods in the heavens,
　　You know that a crime done with malice was not any part of my fault.
　Yes indeed, if you know it was error through which I was brought to my downfall,
100　And that my mind was deluded, not moved by wicked intent,

9

If I was loyal to his family, as permitted to even the humblest,
    If the government of Augustus was all and enough for me,
If I said in praise that under this leader our times were happy,
    And I burnt incense for my Caesar and the royal princes as well,
105   If this was the spirit within me, then spare me, you gods high above me!
    If not, let the waves as they tower fall down and bury my head!

"Am I deceived? Do the heavy clouds now begin their departure?
    Is the wrath of the ocean abated and changed in its will against me?
Not by chance have I called you but with the conviction that no one
110   Can deceive you, O gods; now bring me the help that only you can."

3

When there rises before my mind the memory of that saddest of evenings
    Which was the last time for me that I was to spend in the City,
When I recall that night when I left so much that was precious
    Even now from my eyes there trickles downward a tear.

5   Now was the light of that day near at hand when Caesar had ordered
    Me to depart from the farthest limits of Italy.
I had neither time nor the heart to gather my gear for departure,
    My feelings had grown quite numb by waiting so long for this day.
I had no care to choose slaves or comrades to go on my journey
10   Or to gather the clothes and supplies an exile needs in his flight.
I was struck dumb like a person on whom Jove's lightning has fallen,
    Who lives and, though he's alive, himself does not know he's alive.

Yet at last it was sorrow itself that drove this cloud from my spirit,
    And finally sense and sensation were restored to my weakened frame.
15 I uttered my last farewell to the sorrowing friends I was leaving
    Who out of many there came to see me but one or two.
My dear wife clasped me who was weeping; she too was weeping in her turn
    As over her cheeks undeserving the tears rushed down like a rain.
My daughter was far from our household with her husband on Libyan sea coasts
20   Nor could she have learned of the grief that had fallen to my unlucky lot.
Wherever you looked there resounded the groans and laments of my comrades,
    My household within now seemed like an unquiet funeral.
Women and men and children stood weeping as though at my graveside,
    And throughout the house every corner now had its share of tears.
25 If I may be permitted in a small affair to use larger
    Examples, the scene had the likeness of Troy when that city fell.
And now there grew quiet the voices of dogs as well as of humans
    While Luna above was guiding her nightly team through the sky.
As I looked up at her and above her I gazed at the Capitol Hill
30   Which stood close to my house but whose closeness had been no assistance to me,
I said: "O you powers residing within those neighboring households
    And temples which henceforth forever will never be seen by my eyes,
Gods I must leave behind whom the tall city of Mars possesses,
    Now be saluted in parting for all time to come by me.
35 And although I take up my shield long after I have been wounded,
    Discharge from this exile of mine every impression of hate;
Tell that celestial man what error it was that deceived me,
    Tell him, lest he should believe my fault was rather a crime,
So that which you know, who inflicted my punishment also may know it:
40   When the god has been fully placated I shall be wretched no more."

With such words I worshiped the gods, my wife did so with many more words,
    The sounds of her voice impeded by sobs in the midst of her speech.
For she stood before our family altar, her hair hanging down from her shoulders,
    And touched with her trembling lips the ash that lay cold on the hearth.
45   She poured out many words to the hearth gods, who stood with their faces averted,
    And grieved for her husband, a man whom her words had no power to aid.
And the night as it hurried toward ending gave no more space for delaying,
    The Arcadian Bear was turning on her axis away in the sky.
What was I to do? I was clinging with deep love to my native country,
50   But that night was the last one left to me before my inexorable flight.
Ah, how many times did I tell him who urged me to hasten: "Why urge me?
    Don't you see where you hasten my going, don't you see whence you bid me to go?"
Ah, how often I lied when I told him that I had an hour I'd chosen,
    An hour most ideally suited for such a journey as mine.
55   Three times I set foot on my threshold, three times I called back my footstep,
    That very foot was indulgently slow to its master's intent.
Often I said to them "Farewell," then fell again to much talking
    And kissed everyone for the last time as though I were ready to go.
Often I gave the same orders, then unconsciously I countermanded,
60   As I gazed back over my shoulder at all of those folk I held dear.
Then: "Why do I hurry? It's Scythia to which I am sent" I would falter,
    "It's Rome that I must be leaving: two good reasons to stay.
My wife is denied to me while I live through eternal ages
    And my household and all the sweet faithful who dwell in that household with me,
65   And with them my good companions I've loved with the love of a brother,
    O hearts bound to me with a loyalty like that of Theseus of old.
As long as I may I'll embrace them; perhaps I shall never henceforward
    Be allowed to embrace them further: this hour at least is a gain."

12

Then with speech only half finished I break off my wordy leave-taking
70   And embrace all that's nearest and dearest to this sad heart of mine.
While I speak and we weep in the lofty heavens with a light very brilliant
        A star that is hostile against me, Lucifer, rises on high.
I am divided not otherwise than if my limbs I were leaving
        And part of my body apparently were torn from the rest.
75 So Mettus himself was tortured when torn in contrary directions
        By those horses, the price that he paid for his treachery wrought against Rome.

Then indeed there arises the clamor and weeping of those of my family,
        And their naked breasts are beaten by hands that express their grief.
Then indeed my wife as she clings to the shoulders of him who is leaving
80   Mingled these sorrowful phrases amid her tears as they flowed:
"You can't be torn from me! Together, together we'll travel!" she told me,
        "I'll follow you, wife with her husband, exile with exile I'll be.
The road of our journey now opens for me and the last of earth's limits
        Shall receive me; I'll come, a small burden together with you on the boat.
85 The anger of Caesar commands you to depart from your native country;
        My loyalty orders me likewise; this loyalty's Caesar to me."
Such were the wiles she attempted, the same that before she'd attempted,
        And she scarcely surrendered her conquered hands to harsh reality.
I went out of the house (or was I carried out just like a dead man
90   Without proper funeral?) filthy, stubbly hair over my face.

They told me later my wife was demented with love and with grieving
        And threw herself, only half conscious, down in the midst of the house,
And as she revived, with her tresses made dirty and foul with the house-dust,
        And had lifted her chilled arms and legs up from the floor where she lay,

95 She cried out now for her own person, now for the deserted household,
And often she called out the name of the husband snatched from her side,
Lamenting no less than if she had looked on my daughter or on me
Laid out on a pyre constructed to burn both our bodies in death,
And she wished for relief from sensation of grief by her own bitter dying,
100 Although in regard to her husband she could not escape from her pain.
May she live and her husband, an exile, since fate thus decided his future,
May he live, and his load be made lighter by all of the aid she can give.

4

The guard of the Erymanthian she-bear is touching the ocean
And with his constellation stirs up the ocean afar.
I'm cleaving Ionian waters, however, although I don't wish it,
I'm bold but I am being driven onward by nothing but dread.

5 I'm wretched! How great are the whirlwinds that blacken the water before me,
The very sand is sent upward from the deepest part of the bays!
No less high than any high mountain rise up both stern and the bowsprit,
The wave leaps up to the bowsprit and bathes painted gods in the prow.
The pine-built ribs of my vessel are creaking, the sails scream above me.
10 The keel itself is a-moaning beneath my manifold ills.
The pilot is frightened, confessing his terror by his chilly pallor;
Already he's conquered and follows, he does not guide, the boat's course.
Just as an unsteady rider who's getting no help from his horse reins
Lets them fall on the neck of his horse, rigid and strong, as he runs,
15 So not where he wished to go but where ocean's impetus drives him

14

The pilot, I see, has surrendered the sails of his craft to the boat.
    If Aeolus had not sent out his winds in an altered direction
        I would be driven to regions to which I should never have gone.
    Now far off Illyria's abandoned on the larboard side of my progress
20   And Italy looms in the night, a land forbidden to me.
    Let the wind now cease (this I ask) to strain toward forbidden shore lines
        And let it obey, like me, the dictates of a great god.

    While I speak, and alike desire and fear that I'll be rejected,
        With what a deluge of waves the gunwale's set creaking again!
25 Spare me at least, you great powers who govern the dark blue ocean,
        Let Jove himself be sufficient to vent his anger at me.
    Save my outwearied spirit from a death in the savage waters,
        If now a man who has perished cannot have perished, like me.

5

    O my companion, one never to be mentioned after any others,
        And one to whom in particular my fate is as though it were his,
    The first I remember, most dear, who when I lay thunder-stricken
        Dared to bring aid to me and cheer me up with his words,
5   Who gently gave me his counsel and a reason for living hereafter
        When there was love in my heart for nothing but miserable death:
    You'd know well to whom I speak, although I'd use signs, not his real name;
        My sense of duty would not escape your notice, my friend.

    These things will always remain deep set in the core of my spirit;
10   Forever and ever I'll be in debt for my life to you.

15

My spirit shall sooner depart into empty air and then vanish
    And on a burning pyre my bones melt away into death
Than shall oblivion cancel your kindnesses out of my memory
    And a long daytime of years abolish my gratitude.

15   May the gods be kindly to you and present you a lifetime of fortune
    That lacks no goodly resource, one that's far different from mine.
If, however, this boat should be borne by a wind that is friendly,
    Perhaps the world would not learn of the faith you repose in me.
Pirithous would never have found such a friend as he found in Theseus
20   If he had not while alive gone down to the waters of Hell.
So that your Phocian friend might prove an example of true love,
    Your Furies, O sad Orestes, brought it to pass for you.
If Euryalus had not fallen among his foes, the Rutulians,
    The glory of Nisus, the son of Hyrtacus, would have been vain.
25   Just as of course the yellow gold is proved such in a fire
    So a man's faith meets its test in the fire of difficult times.
As long as the face of Dame Fortune is serene and smiles on us gently
    Everything follows our will in a stream of unlimited wealth.
But once it has thundered above, they flee, and there's no one who knows you
30   Out of the troop of your friends who just now surrounded you.
These were the samples collected from men of earlier ages;
    Now I have found them truthful, based on my personal ills.
Scarce two or three are surviving from so many friends that were once mine
    The rest of them followed Dame Fortune, were never concerned with me.

35   Then all the more, O you few faithful, rush up to relieve my bad fortune
    And give to your shipwrecked companion the security of the shore;

Don't be afflicted with false dread nor fear that your service to me
  May convince that god that your friendship means disloyalty to him!
For often he's even applauded the faith held among those who fought him;
40 Among his own men Caesar loves it, approves it among his foes.
My cause is the better founded since I did not cherish rebellion
  In arms but deserved my exile through my sheer stupidity.
Be vigilant therefore, I beg you, watch over my fate and my future
  To learn if divinity's anger can in any way be made less.

45 If anyone wishes to learn all the facts of my luckless position
  He's asking for more than the circumstances allow him to know.
So many ills have I suffered as stars that shine up above us,
  As many as on the dry sea shore there lie tiny grains of sand.
Many and greater my sufferings than men can know or believe they
50 Were possible; although I've suffered they repose no faith in my words.
A certain share of my sorrows must die in silence when I die;
  I should wish that I could conceal it with dissembling duplicity.
If my voice were one that can't weaken, my heart were stronger than brass is,
  And if I had many a mouth and if many tongues were mine,
55 Not even so could I tell in words everything in my knowledge
  Since the subject matter surpasses my power of words to describe.

In place of the Ithacan leader, O learned poets now living,
  Narrate my evil adventures; I've had many more than he had.
Throughout a brief space he wandered about for many a long year
60 Between those Ilian palaces and his Ithacan home.
The wrath of Caesar compelled me to travel seas that are distant
  From each by whole constellations into the Getic bays.

17

Ulysses had faithful companions, a tight and closely knit party:
    All my companions abandoned me as I took my flight.
65 He as a joyful victor sailed for his father's country;
    I, crushed and exiled, am driven far from my fatherland.
My home is not Dulichium nor Same nor Ithaca either;
    No penalty hence to be absent from them in some distant place.
Rome is my home, the location of power, the site of divine ones,
70   She who looks down from her seven hills all over the world.
His was a body resistant, trained to stand hardships, and robust:
    My powers are weak, unavailing, those of a freeman of rank.
He was continually active, in hand to hand combat kept fighting:
    I am accustomed to studies that keep me feeble and slack.
75 A god has laid heavy hand on me, there's no one to lighten my sorrows:
    For Ulysses a warlike goddess stood ready to bring him aid.
Though lesser than Jove is the god who rules on the swollen waters,
    The anger of Neptune assailed him, Jove vents his wrath on me.
Add that the greatest part of his exploits is no more than fiction:
80   There's not a single fable mixed with the tale of my woes.
At last, moreover, he won through to reach his desired homeland,
    Once more he arrived at his acres sought for so long a time:
But as for me, now and forever I'll lack a dear native country
    Unless the wrath of a wounded god can be made more light.

##

Not so much was Lyde beloved by her poet of Claros' island,
    Nor so much was Bittis loved by her poet from the isle of Cos
As much as you cling, dear wife, to my innermost heart and my bosom,

You who deserve a less wretched but not a better man.

5 As though on a heavy timber I braced against you in my falling:
    If I am somehow alive I owe that favor to you.
You bring it to pass that I'm not robbed nor left stark naked by those who
    Have tried to steal from my shipwreck the very planks of my boat.
As a ravenous wolf that is thirsting and eager for taste of blood-quarry
10   Lies watching an unguarded sheepfold in order to capture a lamb,
Or as a voracious vulture a-hunt for a body that's lying
    Wherever he sees it unburied as yet beneath any earth
So someone with no trust at all in my distressing condition
    Could have made off with my goods if you had permitted him.
15 You in your womanly valor collected strong friends to prevent him:
    To them and to you I can never express worthy gratitude.

Therefore you're approved by a witness as pitiful as he is truthful
    If such a witness as this can bear any weight in a court.
Hector's wife does not surpass you in your integral virtue
20   Nor does Laodamia who followed her husband in death.
If you had Homer applauding your virtues in his epic verses
22   Penelope's fame would come second to the praise he would give your worth:
33 You would have first place among the sacred heroines of past ages;
34   You'd be regarded as first in the good traits of your soul,
23 Whether this springs from yourself, made noble without any teacher,
    Because you were given at birth the high character that you possess,
25 Or whether that princess of women whom for years you have cherished
    By her example taught you how to be a good wife
And made you like unto herself by her long care and her training,
    If I may use large examples when speaking of lesser things.

Ay me, I am sad for my songs have no great power to herald
30   And my voice is too small to sing all of the praise you deserve!
If there was ever in me long ago any force, any vigor,
32   All has been lost to me now by my long-standing ills!
35   Nonetheless, whatever my voice can proclaim to praise you hereafter
         I shall sing and forever and ever you'll be alive in my songs.

7

If you are one who has features that resemble mine in your keeping,
         Take from my locks the garlands from Bacchic ivy twined.
These are the fortunate tokens that deck out a happy poet:
         A crown such as this is not proper to rest on temples like mine.

5   Pretend that you don't but listen, however, my best one, to my words:
         You who wear me upon your finger as you come and go,
You carry my image engraved on a ring made of gold that is tawny,
         Where you may see the dear face of your exile, as only you can.
As often as ever you see it perhaps it will move you to question:
10   "How far away from us now is Naso, our comrade and friend!"

Your faithfulness pleases me but my poems are a greater image
         Of me, of whatever sort I send you that you may read,
Describing the bodies of men which were changed into some other likeness,
         The work of their unhappy master which was interrupted by flight.
15   These as I took my departure, together with so many others,
         Sadly I placed on the fire, destroyed them by my own hand.

20

Just so it is told that Althaia, a better sister than mother,
    Burned her son on the hearth in the shape of a firebrand.
Thus I threw my little books, which did not deserve to perish
    With me, my very entrails, on to the flaming pyre,
20   Whether I hated the Muses, as being the cause of my misdeed,
    Or because the poem was growing as yet and only half formed.
Since they have not completely perished but still are existing—
    I suppose because I had copies made of what I had written down—
25   Now I pray they may live to delight the well-spent hours in leisure
    Of readers and that they may as well remind those readers of me.

Nor yet can these poems be read in patience by any reader
    If he does not know that the final correction is missing from them,
That my work was drawn from the anvil before the last stroke was laid on it,
30   The poems I had begun to write lacked a final scrape of the file,
And thus I seek pardon instead of praise, since my praise is excessive,
    If you, my reader, will not be completely disgusted with me.
Take also these six verses, placed where the book first is unrolled,
    If you'll agree that their place must be there where the reader begins:
35   "Whoever you are who take up these volumes bereft of their father,
    To these at least shall be given within your City a place.
And that you may favor them more, they were not given forth by their parent
    But as it were snatched away from their master's funeral bier.
Whatever the faults that remain to his poems from their half-finished condition
40   He would himself have removed if he had been allowed."

8

Backwards from the deep ocean its waters shall flow to their sources,
　　And the Sun with his horses yoked shall run back over his course:
The earth shall blossom with stars, the sky shall be split by the plowshare,
　　The waves of the sea burst with flames, and fire itself give water.
5　Everything nature presents shall be set in preposterous reversal,
　　And not any part of the earth shall hold its accustomed path.
Everything now will be done which once I called beyond doing,
　　And there shall be nothing so strange but we shall believe it exists.
These are the prophecies I now make who have suffered betrayal
10　　By him whom I thought would bring me aid in my misery.

Did such great forgetfulness of me grasp you, O deceiver,
　　And such great fear to approach one who was stricken by need,
That you would neither bestow your glance nor cheer a poor sufferer,
　　Harsh that you are, nor take part in my funeral ceremony?
15　Does the sacred and venerable name of friendship mean nothing to you
　　And does it lie under your feet now as worthless and vile?
What was it, to visit a friend oppressed by a huge weight of sorrow
　　And with your kindly words do your share to cheer him up,
And if you did not wish to shed real tears at the sight of misfortune,
20　　Make up the brief words of a speech at least to comfort his woe
And to say, what even a stranger might say to me, "I am sorry,"
　　To adjust your voice and your face and to do what the public has done,
And at last to look on the features that you'd never see hereafter

Upon the last day he was present and while it was still allowed,
25   Once only forever to speak, as never again you'd be able,
      You would give and receive the same greeting, one single word: "Farewell"?

But others have done it who were not bound to me by any relation
    And showed me just what they felt, with tears falling down from their eyes.
Why, when with daily acquaintance and powerful causes for friendship
30   Over long space of time you and I were joined by our love?
Why, when you knew me in moments of playfulness, serious also,
    And I in my turn knew your lighter moments and heavier too?
Why was it only at Rome you were my friend when everywhere else
    You have been known to me and greeted so often as friend?
35 Has all this fled to the winds, all of it fruitless and empty?
    All of it carried away beneath waters of Lethe?
I cannot believe you were born in the city of peaceful Quirinus,
    A city to which my feet no longer can dare to come in.
But among the cliffs which the left-hand shore of the Pontic possesses
40   Or amidst the wild crags that rise in Scythia and Sarmatia,
And the veins that surround your heart are stiff as the rigid flint rock,
    And your harsh chest has a vein of iron within itself.
The nurse you had once on a time who guided your tender palate
    To her breasts and gave you suck from her nipples: she was a tigress.
45 Otherwise, you would not now consider my plight with indifference
    And I should be obliged to charge you with harshness of heart.

But since there is added to these cruel losses I suffer from fortune
    The fact that my earliest days should not be rightly fulfilled

23

Bring it to pass that I may forget your sinful transgression
50   And with the same mouth that complains I shall praise your kind service to me.

9

You who are reading this book without hostility toward me,
    May you arrive at the goal of your life without injury,
And would that my prayers which are uttered in your behalf prove effective
    Although for myself they were useless to touch and sway the harsh gods.

5 While you are safe and uninjured you will count on a great many friendships,
    But if the times become cloudy you will be left all alone.
You see how the doves come flying to roofs in their cleanliness gleaming;
    A dirty old dovecote will shelter not any birds at all.
To storerooms empty of grain ants never fashion a pathway:
10   There's never a friend who comes calling at houses whose wealth's disappeared.
As shadow accompanies those who walk in the rays of the sunshine
    (And when the sun hides under clouds the shadow flies off again)
So does the fickle mob follow Fortune's dazzling brilliance
    And departs as soon as that glow is covered over with mist.
15 I hope that these samples of conduct I give you will seem to you specious:
    However, it must be admitted they fit my case to a T.
While my affairs stood upright large enough throngs came to visit
    My home, for it was well known although not ambitious or proud.
But once it had suffered a shock everyone shrank from its ruin
20   And cautiously turned their shoulders, retreating in general flight.

That people are frightened by lightning stroke to me is no wonder
    When they see, as it happens, their neighbor's house going up in flames.

But yet Caesar approves even in his most detested of enemies
    The fact that a friend remains constant to friend in adversity,
25 Nor is he accustomed to anger—no other's as moderate as he is—
    When anyone loves his companion though ruined, if he ever did love.
Thoas himself, it is told us, approved when he knew that Pylades
    Was the faithful friend of Orestes, who came from Argos in Greece.
The faithfulness of Patroclus to his friend, great Achilles, was often
30   Praised by Hector himself, who was his Trojan enemy.
They say that the god of the lower world was saddened to look at
    The loyal Theseus, who followed his comrade down to the shades.
When, Turnus, the faith of Nisus and Euryalus toward each other
    Was described to you we can understand why your cheeks dripped with tears.
35 There is also a faith among wretched folk; it is praised in our foemen.
    Ay me, how few are the people these protests of mine will move!

The state of my personal fortunes is now so low that it ought to
    Create such a flood of weeping that never would come to an end.
But my heart, however dejected because of its sorrowful fortune,
40   Is lightened and calmed by the prospect that your success now presents.
For I have seen this approaching, my dearest man, for some time
    While a slower breeze has been blowing that vessel of yours to this point.
If there's a reward for good purpose and for a life without blemish
    No one exists who deserves it more than yourself, my friend,
45 Or whether some person has risen by means of the arts that are liberal,

25

Whatever case you may handle succeeds through your eloquence.
Moved by these considerations I spoke to you very forthrightly:
"A greater stage is awaiting, friend, the display of your skill."
These words neither entrails of victims nor thunder upon the left hand
50   Nor cry of a bird or a bird-flight seen in the sky have declared:
My augury springs from my reason, my guess as to what will now happen:
    Thus have I made my predictions and arrived at my knowledge of things.
And since this is true, I am grateful with all my heart both to you
    And to me that you have not hidden your excellent talents from view.
55 Would that my own had lain secret in shadows of night which are deepest!
    It would have been more convenient that my efforts had not come to light.
And as your hard training in public speaking has brought you successes,
    Eloquent man, so my talents so different from yours have harmed me.

The course of my life is, however, well known to you, and you know that
60   An author's interests have nothing to do with the speaker's art.
You know, my old friend, that from boyhood I dabbled in verse and my poems,
    Although they are not praiseworthy, nonetheless they are my jests.
Therefore as I have not a leg to stand on as I make their defenses
    Likewise I believe that my poems cannot be charged as crimes.
65 Defend them in whatever way you can; don't desert your comrade:
    And where you have made good beginning may you always continue to win.

10

Minerva the yellow-haired guards me—may she continue to guard me!
    My ship takes her name from the painted helmet Minerva wears.

If she uses her sail she runs well under the slightest breezes
     Or if the oars are required she moves well along with their aid.
5   Nor is she content to outstrip her mates in her speedy progress
     But overtakes boats which have sailed beyond her, whatever they are,
And equally cleaves both the billows and quiet waters far distant;
     The planks of her sides do not open, split by the savage waves.
I first came to know her in Cenchreai, a Corinthian harbor;
10   She remains my faithful leader and comrade in perilous flight.
Through so many dangers driven, through waters stirred into storming,
     Under the guidance of Pallas she has been safe on the seas.
Now also may she cleave in safety the straits of the wide Pontic ocean
     And enter the waters she sails for, washing the Getic shores.
15   As soon as she brought me to Helle, the sea of Aeolus' granddaughter,
     And had achieved a long voyage, marked by a slender wake,
We turned our course to the larboard and from the city of Hector
     We came into harbor and made your port, O Imbrian land.
From there, blown on by a light wind, we came to Zerynthian shore lines
20   And our keel tired out with sailing touched land in Samothrace.
A short haul it is from this place for one who is seeking Tempyra:
     Up to this point she followed her master's hand as he steered.

For I had decided to land and to walk through Bistonian country
     While that ship of mine continued to sail through the Hellespont,
25   And she made for Dardania, named from its ancient founder, Dardanus,
     And Lampsacus, safe with your god who cherishes country retreats,
And the strait which is named for a hapless virgin borne through its narrows
     That divides the city of Sestos from the city of Abydos,
And Cyzicos, Cyzicos clinging to the shores of the Propontic water,

27

30 The noble foundation established there by Thessalian Greeks,
And the coasts of the Byzantine land which skirt the entrance to Pontus:
This place is the wide-spreading doorway by which we enter two seas.
I pray that my boat may reach these goals, driven by strong south breezes,
And briskly sail through the midst of the floating Cyanean isles
35 And into Bithynian bays and from there to Apollo's city
Hold on its course till it comes to the high walls of Anchialos;
Thence may it pass to the ports of Mesembria and of Odessos
And then to the citadel named for you, Bacchus, god of wine,
And the settlement they say the exiles who fled from Megara's ramparts
40 Established and gave as a home for their household gods to possess.
From here may we sail with good fortune on to the city of Tomis,
Where the wrath of a god who's offended has condemned me to go.

If we shall reach it a slaughtered lamb shall fall to Minerva
For her kindness: a costlier victim is one that I cannot afford.
45 You also, Castor and Pollux, who are worshipped upon this island,
I beg you, be present and offer twin blessings on my paths,
For by one I prepare to drive through the closely knit Symplegades,
The other will cut with its prow straight through the waters of Thrace.
Bring it about that the winds, since my voyage lies in two directions,
50 Shall favorably blow on the one and no less favorably on the other.

11

Each letter of every word you have read in my entire volume
Was written by me at the time I was making a perilous trip.

Either the Adriatic has seen me writing them meanwhile
    In a chilly December I shivered, crossing its midmost deep,
5   Or, after I passed the isthmus of Corinth with its twin oceans
    On foot and a second vessel took up the load of my flight,
I think that the Cyclades islands that lie in Aegean waters
    Were astounded to see me making verses where ocean roars.

I am now amazed that my talent amid such disturbance of spirit
10   And such an uproar of ocean and waves did not falter and fail.
Whether the right name to call this passion is stupidity
    Or madness, all fear, all my worries, were calmed and relieved by its aid.
Frequently I was left tossing in doubt by the rainy Hyades,
    Often the star of Steropes menaced the sea with its might,
15   Or the guardian of the Atlantian she-bear would darken the daylight
    Or the south wind would drain the Hyades with its evening showers;
Often the boat shipped water, but I with trembling fingers
    Kept on writing my poems, whatever they may be worth.

Now also the rigging is creaking, stretched by a strong north wind blowing,
20   And the curving water is hollowed into the shape of a hill.
The helmsman himself is raising his helpless hands to the heavens
    And asking for help from the stars, forgetting his nautical skill.
Wherever I looked there was nothing except the image of dying
    Which, divided in mind, I'm afraid of and yet in my fear I desire.
25   I shall reach port but I shall be frightened of that very harbor:
    There is more to be feared on the hateful land than there is on the sea.
For I struggle with snares of the ocean as well as the snares of my fellows,
    And both the waves and mens' swords make for me a double-edged dread.

29

I fear that the men will shed my blood in their quest for mere booty,

    That the waves of the sea may wish to win renown for my death.

The shores on the left are peopled with folk accustomed to rapine,

    Blood and slaughter and wars are a daily habit with them,

And although the wintry waves are shaken upon the deep ocean

    There's a storm in my heart that rages more fiercely than on the sea.

Thus all the more must you make allowance, my candid reader,

    For my verses if they fall short of the expectation you had.

I did not write them as once I wrote in my flower garden,

    Nor, dear accustomed couch, do you carry my body now.

I am tossed in the winter's daylight upon the sea's untamed deep water

    And the roll upon which I write is splashed with its bright blue waves.

The obstreperous storm quarrels with me, indignant that I should be daring

    To write while it hurls at my quarters its sharp and menacing threats.

Let the storm conquer the human! but at the same time, I implore you,

    Let me bring an end to my poems and the storm bring an end to itself.

BOOK II

What have I to do with you, you books, my care and my worry,
    I who, wretch that I am, perished because of my gifts?
Why do I seek you again, Muses damned for my wrong-doing,
    Or is it too little to have deserved condemnation but once?
5   My poems have brought it about that men and women desire
    To know me, but under an omen unpropitious for me.
My poems have brought it to pass that Caesar branded my life-style
    And me on account of my *Art*, a book that was published long since.
Take from me my zeal, you will also take away from my life its reproaches:
10   I lay the blame for the damage I suffer upon my verse.
This is the reward that I've won from my care and my midnight labors;
    The penalty that I have suffered is due to this talent of mine.

If I were wise I should hate with justice the learned sisters,
    Those powers of art who do harm to those who cultivate them.
15   But now—so great a companion is madness to my affliction—

31

I strike my wounded foot once more on the stone which I struck.
Just so, I suppose, the conquered gladiator seeks the arena,
 And the ship that was wrecked returns to the swollen waves of the sea.

Perhaps as once on a time it happened to him who ruled Teuthras
20 Thus the same thing will bring both wound and its healing to me,
And the Muse, who stirred up his wrath, may also calm what she stirred up;
 Often poems serve as prayers to win the consent of great gods.
Caesar himself it was once who ordered Italian mothers
 And daughters-in-law to sing songs to Ops, who wears towers in his crown;
25 He ordered them also to sing to Apollo, when games were presented
 Which each generation will see only one time in its life.
With these examples I pray that your anger, most gentle Caesar,
 Shall now by means of my talent become more gentle as well.
Indeed it was just and I do not deny I've deserved your anger—
30 To such an extent all shame has not fled from my face—
But if I had not sinned how could you bestow your forgiveness?
 My fate has given you cause to extend your pardon to me.
If every time that men sin Jupiter should loose his lightning
 Bolts, in a very short time he would become weaponless.
35 Now when he's thundered and frightened the world of men with his storming
 He renders the air clear and pure after the rain is dispelled.
With justice therefore he is called the father of gods and their ruler;
 With justice the wide world possesses nothing greater than Jove.
You too since you're called the father and ruler of your native country,
40 Then act in the manner that god would act since you have the same name.

And thus do you act; there is no one ever more moderate than you are
 Or one who could handle the reins of your empire as you do.

32

You have often granted a pardon to partisans whom you have conquered,
    A pardon they would not have yielded if they had been victors instead.
45 I have seen many upon whom you have heaped riches and honors,
    Men who had lifted their weapons to hurl them against your head.
That day when the war was ended removed your passion for warfare
    And each side bore gifts at the same time into the temples of gods;
And as your soldiers rejoice because they have conquered their foemen
50   So the enemy also has reason for joy—they were conquered by you.
My cause is a better one for I cannot be said to have ever
    Opposed you in arms and I have not joined any enemy force.

By ocean, by land, by the gods who rule underground I swear to you,
    By you whose godhead is present, you a conspicuous god,
55 That my heart has favored you, greatest of men, and yours I have been
    In the only respect I am able to be, within my own mind.
It was my wish that you would be slow to seek heavenly stardom,
    And I was a modest part of the crowd that wished you the same.
And I burned holy incense for you, among many men I was one who
60   Added my prayers to the mass of public prayers in your name.

Why should I mention my books, those too, the cause of reproaches
    Against me, books that are filled with a thousand mentions of you?
Look into my greater work, one which thus far is unfinished,
    Which tells of bodies transformed into unbelievable shapes:
65 You will find therein that I herald abroad your name and its praises,
    You will find I have pledged my spirit without hesitation to you.

Not that through verses your glory will grow greater, not that it has still
    Any space left in which it can grow any greater than it is now.

33

The fame of Jove is supreme, and more than supreme: yet he takes his
70   Pleasure to hear the account of his deeds as the subject of poems.
And when his war with the giants is described in heroic verses
        One may believe he is happy to hear the praise he receives.
Others celebrate you with as great a voice as is fitting
        And sing your praise with a skill that is more prolific than mine:
75 Nevertheless with the smallest offer of incense a godhead
        Is won over as well as with blood of a hundred sacrificed bulls.

Ah! How fierce and too cruel an enemy was he against me,
        Whoever it was who read out of my love poems to you,
When with a friendlier choice and a better judgment he might have
80   Read to you out of my books poems in honor of you!
Yet who could have been my friend in your presence when you were angry?
        Scarcely then could have I not myself been hostile to me.
When a house has begun to crumble and fall into ruin the burden
        Entirely falls toward the part that was the first to subside.
85 When fortune has made first a crack then everything splits into pieces
        And drawn down into the crash collapses under its weight.
Therefore I gained the hatred of men through my poems, and the people
        Put on the face that was needed toward me, the face that was yours.

But, I recall, you approved of me and my manner of living
90   When I rode past on that horse which you had bestowed upon me.
Even if this gives me no advantage, nor gratitude for the
        Fact I've behaved with honor is due me, I've committed no crime.

34

Nor was the fortune of culprits entrusted to me unwisely
　　Nor the task of judgment placed before the hundred-man board.
95　I judged private cases as well without prejudice as presented
　　And even the beaten defendant admitted that I was fair.
Wretch that I am! More than once, if extreme events had not harmed me,
　　I could have been rescued by you and your judgment in favor of me.
The final event proved my ruin and sent my boat to the bottom,
100　One storm that destroyed a craft which so often survived without harm.
It was not a small part of the whirlpool that dashed me into the abyss,
　　But all of its waves and the ocean itself rushed down on my head.

Why did I look upon something? Why did I make my eyes guilty?
　　Why did I become an imprudent witness to forbidden acts?
105　Actaeon unwittingly looked at Diana without any clothing:
　　He fell nonetheless a prey to his own hunting dogs.
As it seems, one must pay for misfortune even to gods in the heavens,
　　And simple mischance finds no pardon from a wounded power divine.
Upon that day of mine when an evil error removed me
110　My little home also perished, a home that had been without stain:
Little it was in the sense that in my father's generation
　　It was well known and in rank not less than the nobility
And marked neither by great riches nor by its great lack of money
　　Whence came a knight celebrated in neither of these respects.
115　Although our house was distinctive for neither wealth nor position,
　　It was certainly not an obscure one, due to my talent for verse.
And although I may seem to have given it fame when I was very youthful
　　Yet great is the name that I carry, renowned throughout the whole earth,

And the crowd of intelligent readers knows Naso and it is courageous
120   To number me with those men whom no one can disregard.

Therefore this house which was favored by the Muses fell under one man,
      But it fell because of a misdeed that was by no means small,
And it fell in such a manner that it may rise once again
      If only the wrath of a wounded Caesar can turn more calm.
125 His clemency is so great when it comes to the punishment chosen
      That the one he has laid upon me is milder than was my dread.
My life has been spared to me and your anger paused short of destruction,
      O great prince who make use of your power so moderately!
In addition, as if the gift of my life were a boon insufficient,
130   You left me my family's wealth, which you might have taken away.
You did not render your verdict by means of a senate pronouncement,
      My exile was not the decision of a judge chosen for this task.
You punished me with your harsh words—just as I deserved, my sovereign—
      And took your vengeance upon me, as it was proper, yourself.
135 I add that your sentence, although it was harsh and unswervingly rigid,
      Was nevertheless a punishment that in its nature was mild:
For indeed I was mentioned within it as "relegated," not "banished,"
      And the words that contained my fate were ones that spared me as well.

In fact, for a sensible person and one who has powers of reason
140   There is no hurt more severe than to have displeased such a man;
But a mighty power at whiles can be prevailed on to soften:
      When the clouds have been driven away a beautiful day will result.
I have seen an elm that was loaded once more with the leaves of a grapevine

Which earlier had been struck by the savage lightning of Jove.
145 Although you forbid me to hope, I shall persist in hope nonetheless;
　　This one thing I can do although you forbid it to me.
A great hope comes upon me when I look at you, gentlest sovereign,
　　And that hope falls once more when I look upon what I have done.
And just as the winds that blow wildly out on the deeps of the ocean
150 　　Blow not with an equal madness nor with continuous rage
But occasionally drop into silence and, interrupted, lie quiet,
　　And you would suppose they have laid by the power with which they blew:
Such are my fears as they vary, as they retreat in recurrence
　　And give me the hope to placate you, then straightway deny it again.

155 Therefore, by gods upon high who may give and will give to you
　　A life that is long if only they are fond of the Roman name,
By the fatherland which is secure and safe while you are its father,
　　Of which, as among the people, recently I was a part—
Thus to you who always deserve it because of your deeds and good favor
160 　　May the love of a grateful city be given always to you.
Thus may Livia spend with you the years of her marriage,
　　Who, without you, would find none worthy of marriage with her.
If she did not exist, a bachelor life would befit you
　　And there would be no other woman whose husband you could have been.
165 And so may your son be preserved while you are preserved and in due time,
　　An old man, rule over your empire while you, the elder, hold sway.
And may your descendants rival your deeds and the deeds of your offspring
　　Just as they do at the moment, those zodiac figures of youth.
And so may Victory, whose habit is always to rest in your camp ground,
170 　　Now also present herself to you and seek standards well known to her.

37

And around the Italian leader she'll fly with accustomed pinions
    And place on his shining hair the laurel wreath as a crown.
By means of him you wage war, it is in his person you battle,
    To him you give the protection of auspices and of your gods.
175 And while with half of your presence you carry on City commitments,
    Half of you lives at a distance and carries on terrible wars.
Thus may he come back to you a victor, the enemy conquered,
    And tall in the saddle shine forth with his horse which is garlanded too.

Spare, I beg you, your lightning, your frightening weapons chasten,
180   Ah, all too well known to wretched me are those weapons of yours!
Spare me, O fatherland's father, nor unmindful of this appellation
    Take from me the hope that sometime I may placate your wrath!

I do not beg to return, although we're allowed to conjecture
    That often the great gods have granted petitioners more than they asked;
185 If you give me a milder exile and one not too far from my homeland
    My punishment thus will be lightened, a large share of it taken away.
Cast among hostile people I suffer the ultimate ruin,
    Nor is any exile sent farther away from his fatherland.
I am the only one sent where the seven-mouthed Danube empties,
190   Pressed down on my head is the icy wain of the Parrhasian girl;
For Ciziges and Colchians and for the Materean throng and for the Getae
    The Danube waters provide no genuine boundary from us,
And although for a graver cause others have been sent into exile by you
    No farther land has been given to anyone else than to me.
195 Farther than this there is nothing save hostile people and cold air
    And the waves of the ocean that grow stiff and finally turn into ice.

38

The Roman share of the left shore of the Euxine extends to this region:
    The Bastarnae and the Sauromatae hold the adjacent lands.
This region is the most recent to come under Italian rulers
200   And scarcely adheres to the margin of your empire over the world.
Hence I implore that you send me into a safer location
    Lest with my fatherland also my peace be taken from me,
Lest I fear peoples the Danube barely removes from Rome's holdings
    Or I, still your citizen, fall into the hands of your foes.
205 It is right before heaven to keep one who's born of Latian blood lines
    Out of barbarian fetters so long as a Caesar's alive.

Although it was two sins that ruined me, my poem and my grave error,
    I must keep silence concerning the fault of one of these deeds:
For I am not worth the reopening, Caesar, of wounds which are yours;
210   For you to have suffered them once is itself much more than enough.
There remains the second offense, by which "having read a foul poem,"
    I am charged with being "the pander of a shameless adultery."

Hence is it right before heaven for celestial minds to be hoodwinked?
    Yet many things are not worthy to be paid attention by you.
215 Thus Jupiter has not the leisure as he watches both gods and the heavens
    To give his attention or thought to matters of little import.
Thus as you gaze at the world that depends for its safety upon you
    Lesser concerns flee away while you turn to more serious cares.
Should you then abandon your station as head of the Roman empire,
220   Fall to reading poems that are written in uneven meters by me?
The weight of the Roman name presses not in this manner upon you
    Nor carried upon your shoulders appears to be such a light load

39

That you can divert your powers to notice my clumsy triflings
    And examine by careful perusal the poems my leisure produced.
225 Now you must conquer Pannonia, now the Illyrian seacoast,
    Now it's the Raetian army that threatens, the Thracian as well,
Now it's the Armenian seeking your peace, now the Parthian rider
    Stretches his bow or now offers the standards once captured through fear.
Now Germany finds you're still youthful by means of your warrior offspring,
230   And a Caesar makes war in behalf of another great Caesar at home.
Briefly, in such a large body of empire that never was witnessed
    Before our time there's not a single part that is shaky and weak.
The City as well makes you weary, the watchful care of its statutes
    And behavior, which you desire to make similar to your own.
235 The peace you provide for the nations does not fall to your own lot
    And you carry on wars with the wicked without any rest for yourself.
Should I wonder therefore that beneath the weight of such mighty affairs
    You have never devoted a thorough reading to my playful poems?
But if, as I'd prefer, there had been some leisure time for you by chance
240   You would have read nothing offensive in the lines of my *Art of Love*.
It is, I admit, not a poem written in serious manner,
    Nor is it a poem that's worthy of reading by so great a prince:
In spite of this, nevertheless, my *Art* does not break Roman law codes,
    Nor would it induce a young Roman girl to transgress those laws.
245 And lest you have doubts as to what kind of readers I wrote for, the volume
    (One roll of the three rolls that form it) bears these four verses in front:
"Keep off at a distance, you women who wear thin fillets, the sign of
    Your chastity, you who wear garments whose borders hang down to your feet
We sing only what is permitted, of playful thefts that are conceded
250   And in the poem I have written there's nothing that will give offense."

40

And have I not rigidly ordered to keep away from my *Art* poem
    Those women the stole and the fillets they wear forbid them to read?
"Yes, but a well-behaved matron can employ arts which to her are alien
    And the danger remains of temptation although she may not have been taught."
255 Then let the matron read nothing because if she reads any poem
    She can *ipso facto* discover the way to delinquency.
Whatever she reads, if she's anxious the least bit to practice misconduct,
    Will instruct her and fashion her morals toward the pursuit of vice.
Should she take up the *Annals* of Ennius—and nothing's more shaggy than they are—
260   She'll read, of course, how our parent Ilia came to be born.
Should she take up "Aeneadum genetrix," the very first thing she will ask
    Is: "Who was 'Aeneadum genetrix'? And whence came 'alma Venus'?"
I might pursue the point further, taking in turn every genre,
    To show that each kind of a poem can harm the morals of men.
265 Not every book will, however, be subject to blame for offending:
    There is no profit in something which cannot do harm as well.
What is more useful than fire? But if one prepares to burn houses
    He makes his hands bold with fire and fits them with firebrands.
Medicine sometimes removes a man's health, sometimes gives it back to him;
270   It shows us which herbs are of value and which are harmful to us.
Both bandit and cautious traveler gird on a sword as they travel:
    The former wears his to attack with, the latter wears his for defense.
The orator's art is acquired for winning cases in courtrooms;
    You can use it to protect a rascal or harass an innocent man.
275 And so with my poem, if you read it in exactly the right disposition,
    You will find, I am sure, that there's nothing in it to harm anyone.
"But someone may be tempted": whoever has this view is mistaken
    And attributes too much to my writings, reads into them things that aren't there.

41

Yet, nevertheless, I'll admit it: stage plays can scatter the seedlings
280   Of vice: then order all stage plays and theaters to be destroyed!
How often to many is given the chance to be stirred up to sinning
          When sand from the field of Mars is spread out upon the hard soil!
Then do away with the Circus: its license is not without danger:
          It allows a young girl to sit down beside a man unknown to her.
285   When women go strolling at evening for no other reason than this one,
          To keep an appointment with lovers, why are not all porticos closed?

What place is more chaste than a temple? Let a woman avoid it completely
          If there's any resourceful enough to get herself into a mess.
If she stands in the temple of Jove, in the temple of Jove she'll remember
290   How many mortal women that god made pregnant with young.
If she worships in Juno's temple nearby, it will make her remember
          For how many concubine women Jove caused his wife Juno to grieve.
When she looks at the temple of Pallas, she asks why that virgin goddess
          Raised up her son Erichthonius, born out of wedlock in sin.
295   If she comes to the temple founded in honor of you, Mars the mighty,
          She'll see Venus there, joined to Mars, her husband in front of the door.
If she sits in the temple of Isis she'll ask why the daughter of Saturn
          Drove Isis across the Ionian Sea and the Bosporus.
When she thinks of Venus she'll also remember Anchises the hero,
300   And the hero of Latmus with Luna, and Iasius whom Ceres loved.

Each temple can corrupt minds that have been already perverted
302   And yet each one remains safely in the place where it always has been.
305   And whatever woman breaks in where a priest forbids her to enter
306   Is guilty herself of the crime from which the priest is absolved.

42

303 And far from my *Art*, which is written for no one but prostitute readers,
304   Its first page removes the chaste fingers of Roman women of rank.
307 But it's not a criminal action to browse through books of love poems;
    Chaste women may read many things which they're not permitted to do.
Often a lady may look with high-arching brows at nude women
310   Who stand about and perform all the acts of Venus' rites.
The eyes of the Vestal virgins may gaze at a prostitute's body
    While no punishment comes to the pimp who is the master of it.

But why is the Muse of my poems too full of erotic pleasure,
    Or why is it my book that persuades anyone else to make love?
315 There's nothing that I must confess to except one clear fault, just one sin.
    All that I grieve for is that I possess both talent and taste.
Why don't I instead write about the city that fell to Greek weapons,
    Why isn't it Troy that is harassed once more in the lines of my poem?
Why have I kept silent about Thebes and the mutual wounds of its brothers
320   And the seven gates of the city, each with a leader its own?
Nor has Rome, the warfaring leader, denied me matter for verses
    And it is a task for a loyal poet to write of her deeds.
Finally, since you have filled the world with your exploits so famous,
    Caesar, from many a subject there's one at least I must sing,
325 And as the rays of the flaming sun draw everyone's glances
    Thus should your deeds have drawn my soul to a loftier height.

I'm criticized though I am blameless; it's a slender field that I'm plowing;
    The praise of your deeds would require a plow-land far richer than mine.
If some little craft is contented to venture upon a small lagoon
330   It ought not therefore in its rashness trust itself to the broad sea.

Perhaps—but I doubt it—I'm fitted sufficiently for verse that's written
  With lighter themes, and my talents are suited to minor poems:
But if you should bid me to sing of Jove's fiery defeat of the Giants
  The very attempt to describe it would weaken me under its load.
335 A richer talent's required to hymn Caesar's mighty adventures
  Lest the very extent of his exploits should crush my attempt to perform.
And yet I did try; but it seemed I was only detracting from your own
  Great glory, which was sacrilegious and damaging to your powers.
Back to my small undertakings, to the poems of my youth I turned backward,
340 And I stirred my poetic emotions with the image of a false love.
Not that I wished to do this, but my fate drew me on to the climax,
  And I was ingenious to fashion the punishment given to me.
Ay me, where was it I learned how? Why did my parents teach me?
  Why did my eyes ever dwell on the letters, my ABCs?
345 This wantonness made me an object of hatred to you, because my *Artes*
  You believed were designed to entice one to engage in adultery.
But brides did not learn through my teaching to deceive their husbands with lovers
  Nor can one who knows very little of such things teach anyone else.
And so I wrote poems for amusement and lighthearted songs about loving
350 Yet in such a way that no scandal attached itself to my name.
Nor is there among the plebeians a husband who can be uncertain,
  By fault of mine, that he's really the father of his own child.
Believe me, my life-style and morals are far from the poems I have written—
  My life is both chaste and moral, my Muse is an off-color wench—
355 A large part of my work is mendacious and made up out of whole cloth:
  It has allowed itself far more than its author allows to himself.
A book is by no means the index of any man's soul, but a desire
  That is honest can draw from it very much that may charm one's ears.

44

Accius might have been a terror, Terence a parasite bondslave;
360   Those who write about fierce wars might have been warlike themselves.

Finally, I'm not alone in writing of amours so tender:
      I'm simply the only poet punished for writing of love.
What did the Teian Muse of the old man Anacreon teach him
      Except to mix love in profusion with many a cup of wine?
365   What did Sappho of Lesbos teach except love to her girl-friends?
      And yet she was safe for a reader and Anacreon was safe as well.
Nor did it harm you, Callimachus, that you often revealed to your reader
      The lovely boys you were fond of, describing them in your verse;
To jolly Menander a play is no play without its love affairs
370   And yet he is read by the young set, including both boys and girls.
The *Iliad* itself, what is it but a story of adulterous lovers,
      Of a quarrel between a wronged husband and the man who's in love with his wife?
What starts it off but a passion for Briseis, the captured slave girl,
      Which sets the two angry leaders of the Greeks into mutual strife?
375   Or what is the *Odyssey* if not the tale of a woman beleaguered
      In love by a pack of suitors while her husband lingers abroad?
And is it not Homer who tells us how Venus and Mars were bound closely
      And their love-entwined bodies entangled upon the bed of their lust?
Whence but from Homer's pages could we learn as a truth that's unshaken
380   That two of the goddesses fell in love with a mortal guest?

The serious tone of tragedy surpasses that of other genres:
      Its subjects always include the story of love as well.
Does Hippolytus deal with aught else than his stepmother's blind love for him?
      Canace is famed for the love she had for her natural brother.

45

385   What? Did the chariot yoked with Phrygian horses not carry
        The Tantalid, ivory-shouldered, Love driving him on, to Pisa?
    Sorrowful madness stirred up from an injured love made a mother
        Stain a sword with the blood of her children slain for revenge.
    Love changed a king, his beloved, and a mother who weeps for her offspring
390   Itys today, in a moment, into a group of birds.
    If her incestuous brother had not loved his sister Aerope
        We would not read how the Sun god turned his horses away.
    Impious Scylla would not have trodden tragedy's platform
        Unless in her love she had cut off her father's lock of long hair.
395   You who read of Electra and Orestes frantic with madness,
        Read of the crime of Aegisthus and the daughter of Tyndareus.
    What shall I say of the frightful conqueror of the Chimaera
        Whom a deceiving hostess almost did unto death?
    What shall I say of Hermione, what of Schoeneus' daughter,
400   And of you, the priestess of Phoebus, beloved by Mycenae's chief?
    What of Danae, Danae's daughter-in-law and the mother of Lyaeus,
        Of Haemon and of the woman for whom two nights merged into one?
    Of the son-in-law of Pelias, of Theseus, and of the Pelasgi
        Him who was first of the Greeks to set foot on Trojan soil?
405   Let me add Iole and the mother of Pyrrhus, and Hercules' wife,
        Let me add also Hylas and the Trojan boy Jupiter loved.
    I should run out of time if I tried to list all tragic love affairs
        And the rolls of my book would scarcely contain just the names themselves.

    There's a form of tragedy mingled with mirth that is really salacious,
410   And it has many words and expressions that overstep modesty.

46

There is no harm done the author who wrote up Achilles the weakling
    And belittled in his mocking verses all of that hero's brave deeds.
Aristides assembled the scandalous tales of Miletus,
    But Aristides was never driven away from his town,
415   Nor Eubius, the man who described how in pregnant mothers the semen
    Was corrupted, he who was the author of a scandalous history.
Nor did he take flight who composed tales of Sybarite life recently,
    Nor the women who could not keep silent about their bedroom escapades.
These writings are mixed with the great works of the learned poets of old
420   And by generous gift of our leaders become public property.
In order that I may not make my defense with overseas weapons,
    The writings of Roman authors include many off-color tales.
As our worthy Ennius sang of Mars with his very own voice—
    Ennius, greatest in talent but lacking the polish of art—
425   As Lucretius explained the causes of fire so swiftly aflaming
    And prophesied in his poem the crash of the threefold universe,
Thus often Catullus, the love-mad, sang of the woman he loved,
    The wife of another to whom he gave the false name Lesbia.
Not contented with her, he made public a series of love affairs
430   In which he himself made confession of his adultery.
On a par and alike was the scabrous behavior of Calvus called "Shorty,"
    Who revealed his amorous exploits in various forms of verse.
What shall I say of the poems of Ticidas, of those by Memmius,
    Who used real names and descriptions, names that were uttered with shame?
435   Cinna was also their comrade, and Anser, lewder than Cinna,
    And the frivolous work of Cornificius and Cato's lighter stuff,
And she who till now was disguised in her books by the name of Perilla

Is now read under a new one, Metellus, your very own name,
He also who wrote of the Argo sailing on Phasian waters
440   Could not keep silent about his clandestine thefts of love.
Not less unchaste are the poems of Hortensius or of Servius.
    Who among writers will hesitate to follow such names?
Sisenna translated Aristides, nor did this work bring him dishonor
    To have found relaxation with bawdy tales while he wrote history.
445   Gallus won nobody's insults for writing about his Lycoris—
    Only because in his drunkenness he did not rein in his tongue.
Tibullus believes it is hard to trust the sworn oath of a woman
    Or in what she says to her husband about himself, for she deceives.
He admits that he taught her himself to fool the guards at the doorway,
450   And now he says that he has been betrayed by the art which he taught.
He remembers that often on pretext of testing his mistress's jewel
    Or her signet-ring he reached out to touch and caress her hand;
And, as he says, he spoke often by means of a nod or a hand-wave
    And drew secret signs on the round top of the table where both of them sat.
455   He tells with what salves from the body a livid bruise is extracted
    Which was made by a mouth that was pressed in passion upon someone's flesh.
He demands, finally, overmuch from an incautious husband, that he
    Should keep an eye on Tibullus if he wishes his wife to sin less.
He knows who it is that is barked at as he wanders about here and there,
460   Why so often he falls into coughing in front of the closed doors themselves,
And he gives many precepts and shows how by what manner of trickery
    The recently married housewives may deceive their husbands at will.
This teaching did not form the basis of charges hurled at Tibullus.
    He is read and he pleases, and he was well known when you became our chief.

48

465 You will find that Propertius teaches the very same blandishments:
         And yet his name is untarnished by the slightest tinge of reproach.
     I followed these men in succession, since circumstances enjoined me
         That I check my candor and conceal the great names of living men.
     I must admit that I did not fear that where so many vessels
470   Had passed with safety just one more would founder and crash in the sea.

     Others have written up handbooks that teach people how to throw dice—
         A pastime which to our ancestors was by no means a trivial sin—
     What the dice are worth when they're counted, which throws total up to the most,
         And how you can escape from the worst throw, the "Damnable Dogs," as you play;
475 What numbers the dice have and how to throw and after one's thrown them
         To advance in the game when the cry comes: "Your die is lying offside!"
     How the "Black Soldier" progresses beyond the fair limit that's set,
         When a die is lost in the middle as it lies between the two players,
     How he who follows may know how to make war and to call back his scouts,
480   Nor to retreat without making sure that his rear guard is safe;
     How a little tablet is set up and fitted with three little pebbles,
         Where the game is to win by arranging all of your stones in a row;
     And the other games—for I will not describe everyone at the moment—
         By which our folk are accustomed to kill time, a precious thing.
485 Look! Someone else sings of ballgames and the different ways you can throw balls,
         This man instructs you in swimming, that man how to roll hoops.
     Others have written their manuals on how to make use of cosmetics,
         This one's an expert on dining and how to play host with *éclat;*
     Another writes books about pottery and which clay is the best to employ
490   And tells us what jar is best fitted for keeping such liquids as wine.

49

Such are the diversions now practiced in the smoky month of December,
    And it never harmed anybody to have written handbooks like these.
Deceived by these writers, I did not compose any sorrowful poems,
    But a sorrowful sentence descended upon the gay poems I wrote.

495   To sum up, I do not see any writer from so many others
    Whose Muse has destroyed him; I am the sole poet like this to be found.
What if I had written mimes, produced laughter with smut and with sexy
    Skits which have always the same plot—one of forbidden love,
In which a clever adulterer appears and adroitly maneuvers,
500   And a wife who is practiced in intrigue gulls her poor stupid man?
The girl who is ready for marriage, the matron, the man, and the youngster
    Look on at these shows, and a large part of the senate is present at them.
It's not enough that their ears are assaulted by incestuous speeches;
    Their eyes are accustomed to suffer many a shameful sight:
505   When the lover has deceived the husband with some new dodge that's outrageous,
    He's applauded, the play is awarded first prize with the greatest accord;
The less good the play the more profit it brings to the poet who wrote it,
    And the praetor pays a high price for such a vile drama as this.
Examine the expense accounts for your public amusements, Augustus:
510   You will read there of many such plays purchased for you at high cost.
You have witnessed those plays and you've often presented them to public viewing—
    So courtly in every respect is the majesty that you bear—
Indulgently, with your eyes, by means of which all the world gazes,
    You have seen on the stage a foul drama whose plot is sheer adultery.
515   If it's allowed to write mimes which imitate mens' vilest actions
    My poems should deserve far less a penalty than they've received.
Or is it the boards of the stage which protect this department of writing,

50

Or is it the theater itself which lends this freedom to mimes?
My poems also are often presented in dance form to spectators;
520   They have often caught and have held your very own gaze as well.

Of course in your palace the pictures of heroes who lived in past ages
      Shine with their bodies painted by the hands of great artists of old;
There also appear the positions of sex play, the figures of loving,
      On some little canvas reposing somewhere around in its nook.
525 And as Telamon's son there is seated, betraying the wrath in his features,
      And as the barbarian mother reveals her planned crime in her eyes
So Venus, all wet, with her fingers draws out and dries her moist tresses
      And appears still dripping with water, the ocean from which she was born.
Others sing loudly of warfare, fought out with its blood-soaked weapons,
530   And some poets sing the great exploits of your ancestors, some sing of your own.
Envious nature's restriction has held me to narrow boundaries
      And given me limited powers with which to practice my art.
And yet that fortunate author who wrote the *Aeneid* to please you
      Brought "arms and the man" to Carthage and bedded him down with its queen.
535 There's no other part of that poem that's read with more relish than this is
      Where he tells how his hero and Dido were joined in an illicit love.
Some time before as a young man he wrote in his pastoral poems
      How Phyllis and sweet Amaryllis made love in the tenderest way.

I too had sinned in the same vein and composed elegiacs on loving!
540   A fault that's an old one now suffers a punishment which is brand new,
And I published these poems at the time when you, noticing what there was in them,
      Watched me ride past very often, a duly selected knight.
Thus what I wrote as a young man without thought it might one day harm me,

Fool that I was, I've discovered now ruins me as an old man.
545 A long delayed sentence has fallen because of an earlier volume
And my penalty comes at a distance in time from its initial cause.

But lest you suppose that all of my work's of a frivolous nature,
I've often spread sails of the largest to belly with wind on my boat.
I have written six books of my *Fasti* and six rolls to hold them together,
550 And each one of them ends with the month whose feasts it describes in detail.
And this work bears written upon it just recently, Caesar, your title,
And to you the poem's dedicated, but my fate interrupted the task.
And I've given the scepter of royalty to the lords of the tragic stage,
And its language is noble and serious as the actor's cothurnus demands.
555 And I've written, although final polish is lacking as yet to the poem,
Of bodies that undergo changes, turning old shapes into new.
If only you could restrain your spirit a while from its anger
And should order it so that you had time to read a few words out of it,
A few words—from the very creation when our world was rising to vision
560 I have carried this work through the ages, Caesar, down to your own time!
You will see how much inspiration you've breathed into my own bosom
And with what deep respect I have sung of yourself and your family as well.

I have never lampooned anybody in biting satirical verses:
My poem has not listed in detail the crimes of any one man.
565 In my candor I've shunned the harsh mixture of wit and sardonic shadows;
Not a single letter is tinged with poison—my laughter is pure.
Amid so many thousands of people and so many books I have written
I am the only poet whose Calliope has injured him.
Therefore I'll wager not one of our citizens will crow over me,

570 And I'll wager as well that for many my lot has compelled them to grieve;
I cannot conceive that there's any who'll triumph over my ruin
    At least if they hear my defense with the candor in which it is made.

May these words and others, I pray you, prevail upon your divine will,
    O father, O care and salvation of your dear fatherland!
575 It's not that I hope for return to Italy, unless perhaps in the future,
    Much later, when my fate in its longueur has softened your harshness toward me.
No. I beg only a safer exile, a quieter dwelling,
    So that my penalty equals the misdeed that laid it on me.

BOOK III

1

"I come timidly into this City, sent here as the book of an exile:
    Reach out your gentle hand, friendly reader, to one who's fatigued;
Do not shrink back lest I chance to trouble your sense of what's proper:
    No verse in this roll of papyrus teaches a person to love.
This is my master's bad fortune: the unhappy man may not cover
    That bad fortune beneath his verses, behind their rhythmical jests.
Likewise that work where he sported to his grief once in his green years,
    He hates and he curses it now, too late to do him any good!

"Look into the contents I carry; you'll see only sadness within them,
    A poem that matches the circumstances from which it arose.
The fact that my poem is limping and sinks with alternate verses
    Is due to the feet of its metrics or to the long journey it makes.
I am not yellow with cedar oil nor smoothed with soft pumice
    Because I'm ashamed to be dressed up more smartly than my master is.
Some letters of my words are spotted and blurred through their lines with erasures;

55

The poet himself spoiled his opus by weeping over its rolls.
If by chance any phrase shall seem written not in choice Latin language
The land where the poet composed it is a land of barbarian men.

"Tell me, my readers, if it's not too much to say, where I must now
20   As a book go here in the City and where seek hospitality."
When I had uttered these words and stammered them out in a whisper,
        I found scarcely one who was willing to show me the way to go.
"May the gods give you what they have not given thus far to our poet,
        That is, the chance to live softly here in your fatherland.
25   Come, lead, for I'll follow you, although both upon land and on ocean
        From a distant zone of the world I come walking my weary way."
My leader obeyed and he told me: "These are the fora of Caesar,
        This is the road which is named from its holy monuments.
Here is the precinct of Vesta, which serves Pallas and its sacred fire,
30   This was the modest palace of Numa, the ancient king."
Then, turning rightwards, he told me: "This gate is the Palatine entrance,
        Here stands Jupiter Stator, Rome was founded here long ago."
While I gazed at each of these landmarks I saw the tall doorposts arising,
        Shining with arms, and a palace I saw worthy of a god,
35   And I said: "Is this Jupiter's home?" for that's what I thought it was truly;
        An oaken crown it was gave me the augury for this thought.
As I learned to whom it belonged, "I'm not mistaken," I told him,
        "Truly this house is the palace where Jove the almighty resides.
But why is the door of it veiled by laurel trees standing beside it,
40   And why does a shadowy tree encircle its awesome wings?
Is it not because this palace has earned its perpetual triumphs
        Or because it is always beloved by the god who dwells upon Leucas?

56

Is it because it is festal or because it makes everything festal?
 Or is it distinguished for peace, the peace that it gives to the world?
45 As the laurel that's always virid with its branches that never droop downward
 Is plucked as a symbol of glory, does it have an eternal fame?
The reason's attested in writing inscribed on a crown made of oak leaves:
 It indicates that by the service of this man citizens were preserved.
Add to those saved, best of fathers, one citizen more, I beseech you,
50 Who lies driven away to the distance an exile at the world's end,
Where the punishment which he has suffered and which he admits was his merit
 Has as its cause not a misdeed but an error which he has made.
Miserable me! I am frightened of the place, of the powerful leader,
 And my letter is shivered with anguish and trembles under its dread.
55 Do you see my papyrus turn bloodless and pale with the color of terror?
 Do you see how my verses are shaken as they move upon alternate feet?
Sometime, whenever it pleases, I beg you, to pardon my parent,
 O house, I may then gaze upon you among the same masters as these!"

Hence in the same direction I am led up the lofty stairway
60 To the glittering temples that tower, the home of an unshorn god,
Where among Greek marble columns alternate statues loom upward
 Of the Danaids and their father, a barbarous man with drawn sword,
There lie spread for a reader's inspection whatever books have been written
 By the learned writers of ancient days and by those of our time.
65 I searched for my brothers, except, of course, for those volumes he'd written
 Which their father would much rather have not ever engendered at all.
While I was looking in vain the guard who was set over these great
 Environs ordered me to depart from this holy place.
I turned to some other temples close to a theater nearby;

57

70 These too as I found were forbidden my feet to enter as well.
  Nor did Liberty's courtyard within her temple allow me to pass it,
    She who was first to shelter books written by learned men.

  The misfortune of our ancestor recoils on his family also.
    And we, his sons, undergo the flight which he suffered himself.
75 Perhaps Caesar will become less harsh both to us and to him
    When his resistance is worn down by the passage of time.
  You gods, I pray, rather you—for I must not beg all of the gods—
    Caesar, be present to me, greatest of gods, as I pray!
  Meanwhile, since shelter within a public building's denied to me,
    Allow me to slip in unnoticed to somebody's private home.
  You, hands of the common people, take up my poems if permitted,
    My poems thrust off in confusion because of their master's shame.

2

  Thus was it also my fate to visit the land of the Scythians
    And the region which lies underneath Lycaon's pole in the north,
  Nor did you, Pierian sisters, nor you, the offspring of Leto,
    The throng of the learned Muses bring any aid to your priest.
5 To me it's no use to write sportive verse though no crime is committed
    Nor the fact that my Muse is more wanton than my life ever has been
  Since many a danger I've suffered both upon land and on ocean,
    And I dwell where the Black Sea lies parching continually under its frost.
  And I who shunned life's harsh action, born to both safety and leisure,
10   Was soft and unable to bear the stress of reality,

Now suffer the ultimate pangs, nor could a sea without harbors
  Destroy me nor pathways which lead far off to the ends of the earth.
My spirit resisted these evils, for my body drew strength from that spirit
  And, faced with intolerable suffering, bore what could scarcely be borne.

15 While, however, suspended in doubt I was tossed upon lands and on waters
  My labors at verse beguiled both my cares and my aching heart:
When at last my journey was ended, the compulsion to travel was over,
  And I had arrived at the land prescribed by my punishment,
I wished to do nothing but weep; the rain fell less than my teardrops
20 Or than the water in spring which drips from the melting snows.
Rome and my home rose up in my mind and I longed for these places
  And for whatever there still remains of me in the City I've lost.

Ay me, why did I so often knock on the door of my grave-crypt,
  But never for all my knocking was that door opened to me?
25 Why did I escape so many sword thrusts and so often threatened
  By storms there was never a gale that struck my unhappy head?
You gods, whom too constantly I find completely hostile to me,
  You who partake of the anger which one god is venting on me,
Stir into motion, I beg you, my lingering fates and give orders
  That the gates of my death should henceforth be closed no longer to me.

3

If by chance you should wonder as you read this letter I'm sending
  Why it was written by fingers of somebody else, I was ill,

Ill at the farthest corners of an unknown part of earth's circle,
    And I was almost uncertain whether I'd be well again.

5   What do you think I feel, lying ill in this horrible region
    That stretches between Sauromatae and where the Getae live?
I cannot endure the climate, I am not accustomed to local
    Waters, and the land does not please me, I cannot really say why.
My house is not comfortable for me, the food when I'm ill doesn't suit me,
10   There's no one to help me by using his god-given medical skill.
There's no friend at hand who's accustomed to while away hours that linger
    By sitting beside me and telling me stories that make the time fly.
Weary I lie where the farthest places and peoples are present
    And now to my mind in my illness appears all that's distant and dear.

15   Although all things rise before me, you surpass everything, my dear wife,
    And you hold by far the greatest place among all in my heart.
I speak to you though you are absent, my voice names you, only you;
    There is no night that approaches without you, there is no day.
They even report that I've spoken so strangely and wildly my speeches
20   That your name was the one I babbled as if I were completely mad.
Though at present my tongue has failed me and clings to the top of my palate,
    Scarcely to be restored to me by the drinking of unmixed wine,
Should anyone tell me my mistress has come, I should rise up to greet her,
    And my hope to see you once more would restore my vigor to me.

25   Thus while I'm uncertain of my life, perhaps you who live in my homeland
    Are leading a pleasant existence there without thought of me?

60

You are not, I am sure: so much, my dearest, is clearly apparent,
  That the life which you lead without me is nothing but sadness for you.

But if the lot of my life has fulfilled all the years which are due me
30 And so swiftly the end of living has hastened its coming to me,
How much would it be, O great gods, to spare a man on his deathbed
  And allow him the favor at least to be buried in his fatherland!
Either my punishment would have been delayed to the time of my dying
  Or a hasty death would have anticipated an exile's flight.
35 A short time ago I could have died with a name that's unblemished:
  Now my life has been given to me—for an exile's death.
And now therefore I shall perish at a distance on shores that are unknown,
  And my fate shall be made even sadder by the very place where it falls.
My body shall not be given to rest on the bed that's familiar,
40 There shall be no one to weep for me when I'm laid in the earth.
Nor shall the tears of my mistress falling upon my features
  Give to my soul while I'm dying a little more time for life.
I shall not give final instructions, nor while the last clamors are rising
  Will there be any hand that is friendly to close my faltering eyes,
45 But without any proper burial, without honors at my tomb site,
  Barbarian soil will conceal this unlamented body of mine!

Will you perhaps when you hear this, completely disturbed in your reason,
  Rain blows on your trembling bosom with hands that are faithful to me?
Will you, extending in vain your arms toward this part of earth's circle,
50 Cry out in your grief the empty name of your miserable man?
Do not, however, with scratches scar cheeks nor tear at your tresses:

61

Not now for the first time, my darling, shall I have been snatched from you.
At the time when I lost my fatherland, then believe that I perished:
That was the first and the gravest death that I was to die.

55 Now, if by chance you are able—but you're not, my best of all spouses—
Rejoice that my many misfortunes are ended at last with my death.
One thing you can do, you can soften your sorrows by bearing them firmly
With a strong heart; a long time you've borne them with a soul accustomed to pain.

And would that my spirit might perish along with my body together
60 And no part of me slip off undamaged from the ravenous pyre of death!
For if beyond death my spirit shall fly to the airy regions
And the teachings on transmigration of the Samian sage prove true,
A Roman shade shall wander among the Sarmatian shadows,
And among the dead spirits of wild men will always linger a guest.

65 Nevertheless, take care that my bones are brought in a small urn:
Thus I shall not always remain an exile even in death
(There is no one to forbid this: the Theban sister disposed in
A grave her slain brother's body though the king forbade him a tomb.)
And mingle my bones with leaves and the grains of amomus balsam
70 And lay them away in a grave that lies on the outskirts of Rome:
Let the traveler hurrying past with fleeting eyes read these verses
Which you will cut in the marble, chiseled in capital script:
"I WHO LIE HERE WAS THE WRITER OF TENDER AND WANTON LOVE POEMS,
NASO THE POET WAS I, WHO PERISHED BECAUSE OF MY ART;
75 BUT, TRAVELER WHO PASS BY, IF YOU HAVE LOVED, DO NOT NEGLECT TO
SPEAK: 'MAY THE BONES OF NASO GENTLY REST IN HIS GRAVE.'"

62

This is enough for my gravestone, but greater than this are my writings,
    A monument more enduring to serve in remembrance of me.
These I am sure, though they harmed me, will give me after I'm buried
80   The name and fame of their author and a long after life.

But you, however, as long as you live bring grave-offerings to me
    And give me funeral garlands wet with the tears from your cheeks.
Although the flame has transmuted my body to nothing but ashes
    They, in the warmth of the fire, will feel your sad service of love.

85   It would have pleased me to write more, but my voice is tired of speaking
    And my tongue which is dry in my mouth denies me the strength to dictate.
Accept then perhaps the last word I may ever be able to utter
    From the mouth of the person who greets you but who cannot receive it: "Farewell."

4

O you who were dear to me ever but especially so during hard times,
    Whose worth became known to me when my fortunes assumed a down turn,
If you believe in a friend whose experience taught him completely,
    Live for yourself and fly far from the names of those who are great.
5   Live for yourself and as much as you can avoid glittering glory:
    From him who is famous the savage lightning and thunderbolt come.
For since only powerful people can help us to climb up to power,
    Should not he rather assist us, he who is able to harm?
The mast which is lowered escapes from the roaring wintery tempests
10   And billowing sails present more to fear than a sail which is furled.

63

You see how a cork in its buoyancy bobs on the top of the water
    When at the same time the close-knit nets sink, contents and all?

If I who advise you had first been myself possessed of this wisdom,
    If I had been warned I should now dwell in the City wherein I should dwell.
15   While I lived to myself, while a light breeze carried me over the ocean,
    My little boat of existence glided through peaceful waves.
He who falls on level earth—though this rarely happens to someone—
    Falls down in a manner which lets him arise from the earth he has touched.
But wretched Elpenor when he fell from the tall roof of Circe's palace
20   Was only a feeble shadow when he met Ulysses in Hell.
How did it happen that Daedalus flew with trustworthy pinions
    While Icarus fell and in falling named the Icarian Sea?
Surely it was that the former flew high, and the latter flew lower,
    For both of them wore on their shoulders wing-feathers not suited to man.
25   Believe me, the man who has lived in retreat is a man who's lived wisely,
    And everyone ought to remain in the confines his fortune gave.
Eumedes would not be childless if he had not had for an offspring
    A fool who happened to fall in love with Achilles' steeds;
If Merops his father had taken Phaethon as his acknowledged son
30   He would not have seen him in flames nor his daughters turned into trees.

You also, beware of ascending always too high in the heavens
    And, I beg you, draw in the sails of all your ambitious plans.
For you deserve without stumbling to complete the course of your lifetime,
    And you are worthy to enjoy a fate that's more happy than mine.
35   You deserve because of the faithful and gentle concern you have for me,
    Because of long loyalty toward me all the good things I wish you.

I've seen you lament my misfortune with just such a countenance also
    As I might believe was my very own appearance in grief.
I've seen the tears that you wept for me falling over my features
40   And I've drunk them in at the same time as I listened to your faithful words.
Now also with zeal you defend your friend who is exiled from homeland
    And lighten my evils which scarcely in any way can be made light.

Live without envy the gentle inglorious years of your lifetime
    And create a circle of friendship with those who are equals for you,
45 And treasure the name of your Naso, thus far his sole unexiled portion,
    And love it; the Scythian Pontus holds all the rest of him.

4B

The land which stretches the nearest to the sign of the Erymanthian Bear
    Holds me, a land that is parched by the chill of continual ice.
Farther to northward lie only Bosporus, Danube, Scythian swamplands
50   And places whose very names are barely sufficiently known.
Beyond them lies no place where men live, nothing but intolerable cold:
    Ay, how close to where I live lie the ultimate ends of the earth!

And far away lies my fatherland, far off is the wife who is dearest,
    And everything there beyond these two that was very sweet to me.
55 But yet they are present beside me, since all that I cannot lay hold of
    In the body may still be observed by and seen with the eyes of my soul.
There wander in front of my vision home, City, and outlines of places
    And attached to each of these objects are my separate experiences.

The face of my wife floats before me as though she were present beside me;
60   It renders my misfortune heavy, it makes it lighter as well:
The heaviness lies in the fact that she's absent; that which makes it lighter
        Is the love that she offers, the firmness with which she assumes her sad lot.

You too, my friends, you cling to my heart in your love for my person,
        Whose names I desire to speak, all of you one by one,
65 But fear and caution prevent me from performing this friendly duty
        And I think that you would not wish me to place your names in my poem.
Before this, you would have wished it, as rather a most pleasing honor,
        To read your names in the text of the set of verses I wrote.
But since that's a dubious favor, each one of you deep in my bosom
70   Alone I will list, and thus I shall give no cause for your fear.
Nor shall my verses refer to friends whose names I have hidden;
        If anyone loves me he must love me in secret still.
Know, however, although I'm removed from you by a vast region
        That you are always at hand and present within my heart.
75 And in what way anyone can relieve somewhat my misfortunes,
        And do not deny to a man who is crushed the faith of your hand.
Thus may your fortunes remain in ascendance and may you never
        Pray in a similar pass, stricken as I have been.

5

The exercise of the friendship between you and me was so little
        That with no hardship at all you could have concealed the fact,

66

And perhaps never bound me so closely within the bonds of your kindness
    Had my little boat found a wind to drive it safely ahead.
5 But when I fell and all others fled from me in fear of my ruin
    And turning their backs upon me denied they had ever been friends
You dared to reach out and touch a body struck by Jove's fire
    And to enter the household of one whose fate was an object of grief.
And thus you offered to me, though not known to me by long acquaintance,
10   That which in my miserable state scarcely two or three had bestowed.

I saw your face in confusion and noted as I observed it
    That your cheeks were dripping with tears and were paler than even my own,
And perceiving your tears as they fell, a tear for each word that you told me,
    I drank your tears in with my mouth, absorbed your words with my ears.
15 And I felt your arms round my neck embracing me so very tightly,
    And your kisses I have received mingled with sounds of your sobs.

Your defense, dear man, I have known, maintained by your force while I'm absent—
    You realize "dear" stands in place of your actual name in my verse—
And many a manifest sign of your favor toward me in addition
20   Which I shall hold in my heart, never to leave it again.
The gods give you power forever to keep on defending your comrades
    So that you may in a manner more favorable yet give me aid.

If in the meanwhile, however, why I am lost on these seashores,
    As one may suppose you will ask—you ask how I'm getting along:
25 I am drawn by a slender hope which you must not take away from me,
    The hope that the harshness of power in a god can be rendered more mild.

67

Whether in rashness I wait or it's right to suppose this will happen,
    Prove to me that what I wish, I beg you, can be realized,
And employ your skill in public speaking to accomplish this purpose for me
30   To show me my prayers may be able to be fulfilled after all.

The greater that any man is the more placable is his anger,
    And a generous heart can contain kindness and sentiment too.
It is enough for a great-hearted lion to bring down his quarry,
    His fight's at an end as soon as his enemy lies on the ground.
35 But the wolf and detestable bears press on while an animal's dying
    And whatever other beast that possesses less nobility.
What greater warrior at Troy do we have than the valiant Achilles?
    Yet he could not endure the tears of old Priam the king.
How great was the Emathian leader's mercy as shown to his foemen
40   Appears from Porus and from the funeral rites of Darius.
Lest I speak only of mortals whose anger grew gentle at long last,
    The god who was first hostile to her became Juno's son-in-law.

To sum up, I cannot abandon all hope that I shall some day be rescued,
    Seeing the cause of my penalty's not a bloody deed.
45 I did not, as if seeking destruction of all things, seek to destroy the
    Person of Caesar, our chieftain, who is also the head of the world;
I have not said anything, spoken what must be concealed by the speaker,
    Nor dropped any seditious words while drunk with too much pure wine:
I am punished because I have seen with innocent eyes a foul action,
50   And the sin which I have committed is to have had eyes to see with.
Not indeed am I able to exculpate myself quite completely,
    But a simple mistake is a part of the crime attributed to me.

68

Hope therefore remains in the future that he will grow softer toward me
    And lighten my penalty by a change in the place where I'll stay.
55 Would that the bright-shining Dawn Star, who announces the sun at his rising,
    With white horse on the gallop might bring me the news that this day has arrived!

6

The pact of our friendship nor its force, O friend of mine who are dearest,
    Not even if you should wish to would you be able to hide.
For while it was possible for us no other was dearer, more faithful,
    Nor in the whole City another more closely joined to me,
5 And this love was so fully attested that it was known to the people
    Almost more than yourself, almost more than myself.
That simple candor of spirit you reveal to your own dear comrades
    Is known to the man whom you cherish yourself as a friend.
You hid from me nothing so well that I was not conscious of it
10   And you gave to my heart many secrets which had to be hidden within.
And to you I told every secret whatever it was I had hidden
    Except the secret that ruined me, you were the sole person to know.
If you had known this secret also, you'd enjoy your companion undamaged,
    And, my friend, I would have escaped exile by means of your sound advice.
15 But that grey-haired sister, my Fate, drew me on to my evil condition,
    Closing off every road to salvation from me, every manner of aid,
Whether I could have avoided my evil by special precaution
    Or whether because human reason is helpless to overcome fate.

69

But you, who are joined to me closely by the bonds of a mutual affection,
    You who are almost the largest share of my wishes and hopes,
Do not forget me, and when you by grace have attained to great power
    Use it for me, I beseech you, the influence which you will wield,
To make the wrath of a wounded divinity gentler toward me
    And to render my punishment less by changing the place where I'll live,
I beg you to do this the more so because there's no crime on my conscience,
    And the source of the charge held against me is only a simple mistake.
It's neither easy nor safe to tell the mischance that befell when
    My eyes were made to be witness to a deed of hideous ill;
My spirit still shudders to think of that moment, as though at its wounding,
    And its very remembrance creates a new sorrow to follow the old
And whatever else that is able to stimulate me to abashment,
    It is fitting that this should be hidden in shadows of darkest night.

I shall say nothing more on the subject except that I sinned, but my sin had
    No gain in view that I sought for, no profit accruing to me.
My crime must be called by its true name, human stupidity,
    If you wish to attach a just label to whatever it was I did.
If this is not truth that I'm saying, find some other place even farther
    For me—and let Tomis be nothing more than a suburb of Rome.

7

Go to salute my Perilla, you hastily scribbled epistle,
    Become the faithful retainer of all of the things I shall say.

You will find her sitting beside her sweet mother, or else you will find her
    Among her books and the writings the Muses inspire in her.
5   Whatever she's doing, as soon as she knows you have come, she'll give over
    And instantly she will inquire what brings you and how am I.
You will tell her that I am still living but in a way I wish that I were not
    Nor have my ills been alleviated by their long delay.
And yet I've returned to the Muses, although to me they were harmful,
10   And I'm forcing fit words to go walking on alternate feet in my verse.

Say to her: "Are you also clinging to those pursuits which we shared in,
    And do you still write learned poems in a style that's not Roman at all?
For nature gave you chaste manners as well as a lovely appearance
    And endowed you with gifts most unusual plus a real talent for verse.
15   I was the first to conduct your genius toward Pegasaean Springs
    Lest your vein of prolific water should shrink and go evilly dry.
I was the first to watch over you in your virginal girlhood
    And as a father to daughter I was your comrade and guide.
Thus if there remain in your bosom the fires that raged there before this
20   Only the Lesbian bardess will surpass your works with her own.

"But I fear now lest my misfortune prove an obstacle to your progress,
    And after what has happened to me your inspiration will fail.
While we could you read your poems to me, and I read mine to you:
    I often served as your critic, often your teacher as well.
25   I was either a willing listener at times to the verse you created
    Or, when you ceased writing, I'd scold you and make your cheeks flush with shame.
Perhaps the example I've shown you, since my poems have done me such damage,

Has caused you to worry lest you should go the same way I have gone.
    Dispense with such dread, my Perilla, so long as no woman who's living
30   And no man either can learn from your poetry how to make love.

"Abandon, my dear learned colleague, your reasons for writing no verses
    And return to your arts and as priestess preside in your temple again.
Your lovely face will be ravaged by the long years as they vanish
    And an old woman's wrinkles will furrow the beautiful brow that I knew.
35 Old age with ruin shall lay hands upon your fair form and your beauty,
    It comes with a step that is stealthy, without any noise at all,
And when someone says, 'She was lovely,' you will at once fall to grieving
    And look into your mirror and cry out, 'This mirror tells nothing but lies.'
The riches you have are but modest, although you deserve much more of them:
40   But pretend that they're equal to incomes which are positively immense.
For of course Fortune gives to whomever she likes and she snatches her riches
    As well: he's suddenly Irus, who was Croesus a short time ago.
Without going into great detail, there's nothing of mortal possessions
    Which does not perish except our talents and riches of mind.

45 "Look at me! Although I've lost my fatherland, you, and my household
    And those things have been snatched from me which could be taken away,
I am nevertheless companioned by my talent and I still enjoy it.
    Caesar can have over this no jurisdiction at all.
Whoever wishes can take my life with his terrible weapon;
50   Although I should die my fame would remain immortal for me,
And while victoriously from her seven hills Martian Roma
    Looks down on a world she has conquered my poetry shall be read.

Flee also, yourself, from destruction in any way that you're able,
  You for whom a happier future may await your poetic zeal!"

8

Now I should like to be riding upon Triptolemus' carriage
  Whence he threw out the new seed into furrows they had not known.
Now I should wish to throw bridle upon the dragons of Medea
  Which she was driving when she fled from your citadel, O Corinth;
5   Now I should hope to put on me feathers of wings that will flutter
  Whether or not they belong to Perseus, or you, Daedalus:
So that I might through soft yielding air fly on with my pinions
  And suddenly look down from heaven on the sweet soil of my fatherland
And see below my deserted home, friends that remember me dearly
10   And look on the face of the woman who's the sweetest of all—my wife.

Fool, why do you wish for these things in vain with your puerile prayers,
  Things which no day brings you, which no day will ever bring?
If you must pray then bow down to the divine power of Augustus,
  And properly worship the god whose majesty you have known well.
15   He is the one who can give you both wings and a chariot that flies far:
  Let him allow your return, at once you will fly like a bird.
If I should pray for this—for I cannot ask anything greater—
  I fear lest the vows which I make should be too modest by far.
Perhaps sometime in the future, when he has been sated with anger,
20   Then I must make my appeal, but still with an anxious heart.

73

This meanwhile is for me like a favor that is all too ample:
    The fact that wherever he likes he can send me away from this place.
Neither the climate, the waters, the soil nor the breezes can please me;
    Ay me! a continual languor presses here down on my frame!
25   Whether infection sets in from my sick mind to my body,
    Whether the cause of my grief lies in the place where I live,
As soon as I touched Pontic regions insomnia vexes me, scarcely
    Does flesh cover up my bones or food give pleasure to tongue.
That pallid color which comes to leaves when they're stricken in autumn
30   With the first chill of the winter when frost has blighted the trees
Possesses my limbs and my strength is restored from no other quarter,
    And never a cause for my plaintive sorrow is absent from me.
My sick mind is in no better state than my suffering body,
    Each of them equally ill, a twin affliction I bear.
35   In front of my eyes there clings just like a visible image
    The shape of my sorrow at hand which I must hide from view.
And when I look at the region, the local customs and life style,
    Their speech, and when I recall what I am now and what I was,
I become so desirous of death that I burst out against Caesar
40   Because in his wrath he did not avenge my affronts with a sword.
But since for his hatred he used a more civilized way to express it
    May he make my exile lighter by letting me change its place.

9

Here also there are then—who would have ever believed it?—Greek cities
    Among the outlandish place-names of an inhuman barbarism;

74

Hither have come likewise colonists sent from Miletus,
    And they have established Greek homes here in the land of the Getes.
5   But the ancient name of the region, older than the city they founded,
    Is proven to have come down from the tale how Absyrtus was slain.

For with the boat which was fashioned by the skill of pugnacious Minerva
    Through waters not sailed in before she was the first, it is said,
To pass over in flight from her parent, leaving her father deserted,
10   Applying her oars to these shallows, Medea the daughter disloyal.
As a watchman from a high hill saw him arrive at a distance,
    "A Colchian visitor's coming, I know the sails," he said.
While the Minyae go rushing, while the rope is loosed on the seashore,
    While the anchor follows the willing hands as they draw it up,
15   The Colchian woman, aware of her deeds and her great wicked daring,
    Struck with an impious hand her breast that deserved its blow,
And, although an immense bravado remained in the mind of the maiden,
    There appeared a pallor of fear on her face as though thunderstruck.

Then when she saw the sails coming nearer, she said, "They have caught us"
20   And "We'll have to delay my father by some kind of stratagem."
While she was seeking what she should do and was glancing about her
    By chance she turned her eyes sidewards and saw her small brother there.
And as his presence was brought to her mind, "We have conquered," she shouted:
    "The death of this boy will present me the means to preserve my own life."
25   At once she stabbed with a stiff sword his innocent side as he sat there
    Quite unaware and not fearing any such deed as this.
And then she tore up his members and scattered them over the farm fields
    Of the land and left them for finding in many a separate place

(And lest her father should miss them, she stuck high upon a cliff side
30   The bleeding head of her brother and his pale little shorn-off hands).
And thus while her father was hindered by each new vision of horror
        And stopped to pick up the boy's fragments, his terrible journey grew slow.

For this reason this place is called Tomis, because it is told us that once here
        A sister cut into pieces her brother's arms and his legs.

10

If anyone still there among you remembers the Naso who's snatched off
        From you, and my name is surviving in the City from which I have fled,
Let him know that I live in the midst of a distant barbarous country
        Placed under stars that never go dipping down into the sea.
5   The Sauromatae surround me, a wild race, the Bessi and Getae,
        Names how unworthy of mention or notice by talents like mine!

Yet while the warm breezes are blowing the Danube protects from attackers,
        This river with its shining waters keeps warfare out of our land.
But when gloomy winter has lifted its squalid countenance upward
10   And the earth has turned into white marble compounded of ice and of snow,
While Boreas opens out toward us and snow dwells beneath Ursa Major
        Then it is clear that these peoples are pressed by the shuddering Pole.
Snow covers the ground; it lies there beyond sun or rain to dispel it;
        Boreas makes it grow hard and almost perpetual.
15   When the first snow has still not been melted a second snowstorm's arriving;
        Snow usually stays here in many places as long as two years.

76

So great is the strength of the north wind let loose upon us that it pushes
    High towers down, makes them level with earth, and rips away roofs.
The people wear skins and stitched trousers to ward off the evil chill winter
20   And from fully covered bodies expose only faces to view.
Often their frozen hair rattles, when shaken, with hanging icicles
    And their white beards gleam in the sunshine with the hoar frost that covers it.
The wine stands frozen, denuded, preserving the shape of its wine jar
    And nobody takes a drink of it but sucks on its fragments of ice.
25 How? Shall I tell you how streamlets grown hard and congealed by the winter
    Are hacked into breakable water that comes from the midst of a pond?

Even the Danube, no smaller than the stream where papyrus is growing,
    Is mingled by many an outlet with a vast estuary.
Even its blue waters harden beneath the stiffening north winds,
30   It freezes and creeks to the ocean under its cover of ice.
And where the boats sailed people walk now and over the waves of the river
    Grown hard with the cold a horse's hooves go galloping on,
And over new bridges beneath which the waters of Danube are gliding
    Sarmatian oxen go pulling their quaint barbarian carts.
35 People will scarcely believe me, but since there's no profit in lying
    One should have full faith in a witness like me who's seen what I've seen:
I've seen the broad ocean lie stiffly, its surface turned into sheer ice,
    While a slippery shell was pressing the motionless waves of the sea.
It's not enough to have seen it: I walked out on the hard icy surface
40   And the top of the wave lay beneath my foot, and my foot was not wet.
If you had had such a footing, Leander, once on a time, then
    Your death would not have been caused by a narrow strait of the sea.
Then curving dolphins are helpless to leap up into the breezes

For if they try it the bitter winter will force them back;
45   And although Boreas whistles with wings as he flaps them about him
            There will be no waves set in motion within the constricted sea;
Ships will stand fixed in the marble-like ice that winter has fashioned,
            And the oar cannot cut through the water which has become rigid with cold.
I saw some fishes that clung there bound firmly within the ice coating
50   And even then part of their bodies stirred with life to my sight.

Whether therefore the savage force of too strong a north wind
            Compels the river at flood stage and the sea waters to freeze
As soon as the Danube is hardened to ice by dry winds from the north land
            The barbarian enemy rides on it with his speeding horse;
55   An enemy powerful with his mount and his far-flying arrow,
            Who lays waste the neighboring country and its soil as he moves far and wide.
Some of the inhabitants flee and leave no one to tend their harvests
            And possessions thus left unprotected are ravaged and stolen away,
The crops of a slender farmland, their herds and their carts that go screeching
60   And such riches whatever they may be which a poor settler owns.
Part of them are taken captive, with arms tied up at the elbows,
            Looking behind them in vain at their fields and the homes they leave.
Part of them fall transfixed in their misery by the barbed arrows
            For each iron arrow head is dipped in a poisonous juice.
65   Whatever they cannot carry or lead away with them they forfeit,
            And the enemy puts to the torch the innocent homes which they owned.

Even whenever there is peace they tremble with fear of warfare,
            And nobody furrows the soil, driving the heavy plowshare.

78

This land either sees or has feared an enemy it has not witnessed.
70   The earth that is left untilled returns to the wilderness.
Here the sweet grapes do not hide beneath the shade of the vine leaf
        Nor does the bubbling must fill up the lofty vats.
This area does not grow apples nor would Acontius have been
        Able to write here those words he sent for his mistress to read.
75   You would see fields without foliage, a land that is barren of tree life:
        Ah, such a region a man who is happy should never approach!

And therefore while the great world stretches so widely around it,
        This is the land that is chosen to serve as my punishment!

11

Whoever you are who exult, you villain, at my misfortune
        And bloodthirstily charge me with crime, endlessly on and on,
You were born upon cliffs, you were reared on the milk of a wild beast,
        And I should say that your heart is filled with pieces of flint.

5   What higher level remains to which your anger aspires,
        Or what other ills do you see not now included with mine?
A barbarous land and the inhospitable shores of the Pontus
        Look upon me, and the Bear of Maenalis with her north wind.
There is no exchange of language between me and this wild people:
10   All of the area's filled with dread and anxiety.
And as the fleeting deer is caught by ravenous wild bears,

79

As the lamb stands trembling with fear surrounded by mountain wolves,
So am I fenced all about and threatened by warlike peoples
      And frightened with enemies pressing almost against my sides.
15 I admit that my punishment's small, to be deprived of my dear wife,
      To be deprived of my country and all who are close to me,
To suffer no evil except the naked anger of Caesar—
      But isn't the naked anger of Caesar enough for me?

And nevertheless there is someone who claws at my wounds, raw and bleeding,
20   And opens his cultured lips to condemn my manner of life.
In a case that is open and shut any person may be persuasive
      And the slightest of powers prevail to destroy what is already crushed.
It takes courage to bring down a stronghold and sturdily standing ramparts;
      Whatever coward who likes can tumble what's ready to fall.
25 I am not the man I was once; why grind a mere ghost into pieces?
      Why hurl your stones at my ashes and at my mortal remains?
Hector was Hector while he was fighting in battle; but Hector
      Was no longer the same when his body was tied to Thessalian steeds.
Remember I'm not the same person whom you once knew long before this:
30   Of that man there now remains this shadow of me and no more.
Why incessantly lash out with bitter words at my shadow, you foul fiend?
      Spare me, I beg you, and cease to harass my spirit in death!
Consider my crimes to be true, all, and nothing among them
      Which you might consider to be an error rather than sin:
35 Look, I have paid as an exile my penalty—appease your heart then!—
      A heavy exchange for my fault and heavy the place of my plight.
My misfortune can seem to be worthy of tears from a hangman in person:
      And yet to one judge—that is you—it has sunk not sufficiently low.

You are fiercer than fierce Busiris, and you are more fierce than he was
40   Who heated with slow-burning fire a bull that he made out of brass
And gave it, they say, to the tyrant who ruled over Sicily island,
          Praising the craft of his work, recommending it with words like these:
"King, there's a practical use in this gift, there is more than an image;
          Not only beauty resides here in the statue I've made.
45   Do you see the right side of the bull where a door has been made that will open?
          Here you must throw someone in, whomever you wish to destroy.
After you've thrown in the person then consume him with slow-burning fire:
          He will bellow with pain and his voice will sound like a regular bull's.
For this invention please balance my gift with a gift of your choosing,
50   Give me, I pray you, a worthy reward for my talent in art."
He spoke, and Phalaris answered: "Marvellous inventor of torture,
          Dedicate your artwork yourself while you are present with me."
At once he was cruelly burned in the fires which he had demonstrated,
          Uttering moans from his mouth, twin sounds—his own and the bull's.

55   What have I to do with Sicilians among Cizigae and the Getae?
          To you, whoever you are, returns the complaint which I make.
In order that you may quench your thirst with my blood at long last then
          And carry away in your greedy heart all the joy you can bear:
I have suffered so many evils on land, so many on voyage,
60   That I think even you would be sorry when you have heard them all.
Believe me, if the woes of Ulysses should be compared with my fortunes
          The anger of Neptune would seem to be lighter than Jove's toward me.

Therefore, whoever you are, do not reopen your charges,
          And take away from my deep wound the heavy hands which you ply

81

65 So that forgetfulness may diminish the fame of my misdeed
        Allow what I've done to heal with a scab that will form over it.
    Remember the lot of us humans, which lifts the same people up higher,
        Then dashes them down—stand in fear of reverses of fortune yourself.

    And since, something which I thought would never be able to happen,
70   You are so greatly concerned about my affairs and my life,
    Know this: there is nothing to fear; my most miserable lot's without danger:
        The anger of Caesar draws off every bad luck to itself.
    In order to make it more clear, lest anyone think I am faking,
        I wish that you could experience the same sufferings which I endure.

12

    Now south winds diminish the wintry chills; at the end of the season
        The Maeotian winter appears to last longer than ever before,
    And the Ram which bore Helle (not safely) upon his back to her haven
        Makes the hours of the night equal to those of the day.

5   Now boys and laughing girls go plucking the wild violet flower
        Which grows in the woods without anyone to scatter its seeds.
    And meadows grow youthful and lovely with flowers of various colors
        And the talkative bird begins to sing with an untaught tongue;
    And in order to ward off reproaches as a bad mother, the swallow
10   Builds under the beams a cradle and a small house for her young;
    And the winter wheat, which lay covered beneath the furrows of grain fields,
        Pushes its tender green shoots out of the warming earth.

82

Wherever the grape vine is planted, buds burst forth on its branches,
    Although on the Getic shores there is no vine to be seen;
15 Wherever a tree is growing, its limbs swell out in the springtime
    Although within Getic borders there is no tree to be seen.

Now you have holidays in Rome, and games given one after another
    Take the place of the garrulous conflicts that fill the Forum with words.
Now people ride out on their horses or play with light weapons together,
20   Now balls go flying and round and round rolls the hastening hoop;
Now after smearing their bodies with dripping oil the young athletes
    Wash down in the Virgin's Fountain their limbs tired out with sport.
The theater season is active, applause rings with partisan zeal,
    And instead of three fora there echo the sounds from three theaters.
25 O four times blessed, as many times happy as no one can count up,
    For whom it's allowed to delight in a City that has not been banned!

But I feel the snow still around me which melts in the springtime sunshine,
    And the water is no longer chopped out in the form of ice from a pond;
The sea does not stiffen with hoar frost nor over Danube as before now
30   Does the Sarmatian cart drawn by oxen come screeching across the ice.

Some ships nonetheless are beginning to make for the land where I'm living
    And foreign vessels will moor their sterns upon Pontic shores.
I'll run down eager to greet the captain and once I have met him
    I shall ask why he's coming, who is he, and from what places he's come.
35 It would be strange if he had not sailed from some nearby seacoast
    And quite safely plowed through nothing except the neighboring waves.
It's possible also that from the mouth of far-stretching Propontis

Someone sails hither depending upon the trustworthy south wind.
It's only a very rare sailor who from Italy crosses the ocean
40   And rarely casts anchor upon our coasts where no harbors lie.

Whether he knows how to speak in Greek or the Latin language—
    He's certainly much more welcome if he can speak Latin with me—
Whoever he is, he is able to bring me the gossip he's gathered,
    To become part of what he tells me and even increase it a bit.
45 He can tell me, good Heavens, about the triumphs he's heard and attended
    Celebrated by Caesar, the vows that he's made to Latian Jove,
And you, Germany, you rebel, who have been brought down at long last,
    How you have lowered your sad head at the feet of that great general.

He who will tell me these current events, which I grieve I've not witnessed,
50   Will become at once my dear house guest to stay as long as he's here.
Ay me, is the home of Naso now only in Scythian regions,
    Pontus, do you give me your country as a shrine for my household gods?
O gods, bring to pass that Caesar shall wish me no regular dwelling
    In these regions, but only a lodging here as my penalty.

13

Look, he is superfluous—for of what use was it to be born?—
    My birthday god at his proper time is at hand again.
Hardhearted, why did you come to the wretched years of my exile?
    You should rather have placed a final limit to them.

5   If you had really cared for me, if you had any shame in the slightest,
        You would not have followed behind me out of my fatherland,
    And in the place where you first acknowledged me, born but to evil,
        There you should have attempted to make it the last day for me.
    And when I was forced to depart from the City you should have acted
10   As did my own companions and with sad face said to me: "Farewell."

    What are you doing in Pontus? Surely the anger of Caesar
        Has not sent you as well to the end of the frigid zone?
    Of course you expect the usual honors that custom requires,
        That a white robe I should be wearing which hangs from my shoulders down,
15 That a smoking altar be decked out and encircled with flowering garlands
        And that grains of incense should crackle on flames dedicated to you,
    And that I should properly offer the pancakes that mark the occasion
        Of my birth, and compose with assenting voice my favorable prayers?

    I am not in such a position, the times are for me most improper
20   That I should show my delight because you have come to me.
    A burial altar's more fitting, encircled with death's gloomy cypress,
        And a pyre heaped up for my body with fires ready to flame.
    I do not wish to burn incense which has no effect on divine ones
        Nor among such dreadful afflictions should my benedictions arise.
25 But if there is something that I should ask for upon this birthday
        It is this: that you never come back again to these regions, I beg,
    While a part of the world that is almost its end, it is named the Pontus
        But falsely called Euxine—its meaning is "hospitable"—holds me.

85

14

You honorable patron and master of poets and learned scholars,
    How does it go with you, sir, who always befriended my work?
Do you take pains as you used to when I was still out of danger
    To praise me now too lest I seem to have vanished completely from sight?
5   Do you take care that my poems are published, except for one poem,
    My *Art of Love*, which brought harm to the man who was author of it?

Yes, keep on doing this, please, you who're fond of new writers of poems,
    In whatever way that you can maintain my "corpus" in Rome.
Exile was ordered for me, it was not decreed for my writings
10   Which did not deserve to suffer the penalty laid upon me.
Often a father is exiled in flight to external seashores,
    But his children are given permission to continue their life at Rome.
In the example of Pallas, who was born without any mother,
    Are my poems; they are my offspring who form my posterity.
15   I commend them to you, my friend, and since they are robbed of their parent
    My poems will become more of a burden to you, their sponsor and guide.

Three of my children are tainted with the illness that brought me misfortune,
    But openly make it your business to take the rest up in your care.
Among these are fifteen volumes that deal with forms that were altered,
20   Poems which were snatched from their author's actual funeral rites.
This work would have had, if I had not perished before it was completed,

86

Its final correction from my hand and have counted on surer repute:
Now it has come uncorrected into the mouths of the people,
      If I may say I am quoted by people in any respect.

25   Add this work, such as it is, to the list of books I have written,
      Which comes to you sent from the very other end of the earth.
He who will read it—if anyone reads it—should reckon beforehand
      As to when it was written and where the poem was written as well.
He will be fair to my writing when he knows the time it was written
30   Was during my exile, the place was the homeland of barbarity,
And he'll be amazed that among so many reverses I could still
      Endure to set my sad hand to the task of writing a poem.
Misfortune has broken my talent; even before it sprang forth from
      A source that was quite unprolific, its vein was a slender one.
35   But whatever it was, it has fled me for lack of due exercisement
      And perished because it has dried up by lying fallow so long.
There is no library here from which I may find stimulation
      And challenge; in place of books, bows and arrows resound.
There is no one in this land who, if I recited my poems,
40   Would understand as he heard and thus be of service to me.
There is no place for retreat; the garrison stationed on ramparts
      And the closed gates of the place keep hostile Getae away.
Often I search for a word, for a name, I search for a location,
      But there is no one to give me the information I need.
45   Often when I try to say something—I'm ashamed to admit it!—
      The words which I seek fail me, I have forgotten how to speak.
I am surrounded almost by Thracian and Scythian language,

And it seems that I could compose my verse in the Getic tongue.
Believe me, I fear that you may read Sintian words mixed with Latin,
50   And in my writing as well Pontic words you may find.
Then honor my book with your pardon, whatever the book may be to you,
And excuse it because of my fate and the special condition I'm in.

BOOK IV

1

If you shall find many errors, as I know you will find, in my volumes,
    Consider them due to the time when, reader, they were composed.
I was an exile and I sought, not fame, but for peace and quiet
    That my mind should not be intent forever upon its ills.

5   This is why even the digger of ditches sings though he's shackled
    And softens his weary labor with an artless melody.
He sings also who bends his back toward the slimy sandbar,
    Dragging the sluggish barge with difficulty upstream.
And he who draws the slow oars to his breast in an even rhythm
10   Makes in time with his arms his strokes on the splashing waves.
When the tired shepherd leans on his staff or sits down on a boulder
    He soothes the sheep which he tends with a song he plays on a reed.
At times the servant girl sings, at times does the task she's allotted,
    And thus with her song beguiles and deceives the labor she does.
15   They say that grief-stricken Achilles when Briseis had been taken from him

89

Lessened the cares of his heart with his Thessalian lyre.
While Orpheus drew with his song hard rocks and the forests behind him
   He mourned for the wife he had lost, snatched from him a second time.

20
The Muse relieves me as well on my way where I'm ordered in Pontus;
   She was the only companion to stay with me during that flight.
She alone does not fear ambush or Sintian swordsmen
   Nor ocean nor winds from the sea nor this land of barbarians.
She also knows, when I perished, what error it was that deceived me,
   And that there was a fault in my deed, that what I did was no crime.
25
Of course, now she's fair to me although before she was hostile,
   When she was a culprit with me, charged, as I was, with a crime.

I could well wish I had not, since they were to be harmful to me,
   Placed my hands on the sacred objects of the Pierian girls.
But what now am I to do? The power of their ritual holds me
30
   And although I was harmed by a poem I'm madly in love with verse.
Thus did the exotic lotus please the palates of men from Ithaca,
   Its savor was grateful to those whom it was destined to harm.
The lover feels that which destroys him but nevertheless he clings to it
   And persists in pursuing the object of his affectionate guilt.
35
I too take pleasure in reading books, although they brought evil,
   And I am in love with the very weapon that caused my wounds.

Perhaps this zeal may appear to be to you only a madness,
   But even this madness possesses a certain utility:
It keeps me from constantly brooding upon the misfortune that's pressing
40
   And renders my spirit unmindful of the sorrowful state I am in.

As the injured Bacchante's oblivious of the wound for which she has no feeling
    While she howls to the point of exhaustion among the Idaean crags,
So when my bosom warms up with the touch of the ivy-crowned thyrsus
    My spirit soars to a realm that is higher than human ills.
45   It has no feeling of exile nor shores of the Scythian ocean,
    It does not perceive the anger which the gods hold for me.
And as though I were drinking the potion of Lethe's forgetfulness
    When I am inspired all sense of my sadness and suffering is gone.
With justice therefore do I worship the goddesses who bring me surcease,
50   Companions from Helicon with me during an exile's flight,
Who deigned to accompany me partly on sea and partly on dry land
    And to follow me either on shipboard or when I went upon foot.

Let them at least be gracious toward me, I beg, for the rest of
    The gods form a pack that's united together with Caesar the great,
55   And heap up as many misfortunes against me as shores have their sea sands,
    As many as ocean has fishes, as many as fish have eggs.
In spring you will number the flowers, in summer the heads of the wheat ears,
    The fruit that grow ripe in the autumn, the snows in the winter chill
Before you will number my sufferings, as I knocked round in the whole world
60   While in my wretchedness I made for the left-hand shores of Euxine.

Not that, however, my troubles are less here since I have landed:
    My misfortune has followed my path to this place as well;
Here also I am quite conscious of the natal threads of my fortunes,
    Threads which are spun out of black wool, a sign of disaster for me.
65   And not to tell all of the dangers or perils besetting my safety,
    All of them true, understand me, but harsh beyond any belief,

What wretchedness is it to live here among the Bessi and Getae
    For him who was always a byword upon the lips of the folk!
How terrible is it to seek protection through gate and through ramparts,
70   And to scarcely find safety through even such defences as these!
As a young man I shunned the fierce combats that mark military encounters
    And exercised only with weapons that people use mainly for sport;
Now that I'm old I strap on my side both sword and a buckler
    And place on my head a war helmet to rest there upon my grey hairs.
75   For as soon as the scout from his tower has given the sound of alarum
    Straightway I put on my armor and weapons with trembling arm.
The enemy taking his bow and arrows dipped into poison
    Savagely rides up and down the walls with his panting horse.
And just as the ravaging wolf who captures a lamb who was slow to
80   Hide in the fold and he drags him through forests and fields away,
Thus anyone who was unable to enter the gates of the city
    If the barbarous enemy finds him among the fields, he is lost:
Either he follows, a captive, with chains hanging round his collar
    Or, shot with a poisoned arrow, he falls to the ground and dies.

85   Here then I lie, a new settler in a place that is quite full of danger:
    Ay, too long is the lapse of time to complete my fate!
And yet the Muse, who's my guest, is able to turn to her verses
    And her ancient poetic ritual among such misfortunes as these!
But there is no one to recite to nor one to receive my poems
90   With his ears or to understand their Latin language as well.
And so to myself—what else can I do?—I write and I read them
    And my writing is safe from the critic, for that critic is myself.
Nevertheless I keep saying: "For whom do I lavish this labor?

Shall Sauromatians read my writings or shall it be Getes?"
95 Frequently also I shed tears that fall upon what I am writing
And the letters set down on papyrus are moist with the flow of my grief,
And my heart recognizes its old wounds as though they were something novel
While the flood of my weeping runs into the folds of my garment like rain.
But when I have come to my senses and recall who I am, who I have been,
100 And there comes to my mind whence and whither misfortune has carried me on,
Often my hand in its madness and anger with verse and its own self
Has thrown my verse into the fire to burn like a corpse in the flame.
And so, since not many of my poems survive from so many others
Be tolerant toward them, whoever you may be, whenever you read.
And accept in good part my verses, no better than what I'm enduring,
O Rome so far in the distance, a city forbidden to me!

2

Now fierce Germany, like all the world, is conquered at long last
And bends her knee in submission to Caesar and to his house,
And the lofty palaces on their high hill are veiled with garlands
And incense crackles on fire and its smoke obscures the day,
5 And the snow-white victim led up to the altar offers its bowed neck
To the stroke of the axe and sprinkles the earth with its scarlet blood.
And the gifts which they have promised to the temples of gods who are friendly
Each of the Caesars as victor is now preparing to bring,
And the young men who bear the name of Caesar are growing to manhood
10 In order that this house may govern forever over the world.
Livia with her good daughters-in-law for the safe homecoming

93

Of her son offers gifts to the gods who deserve them, and often will give;
And together the Roman matrons and the women who live without sinning
Are tending the sacred fires in perpetual virginity.
15 The loyal people rejoice, with them the Senate rejoices,
And the knighthood as well, of which I was recently a modest part.
I miss the general rejoicing, an exile driven far from Rome,
And only the faintest echo of it now reaches my ear.

Then all the folk will be able to watch as the triumphs are passing
20 And read names of captured cities, the titles their leaders possessed,
And kings wearing chains on their captive necks the people will look at
As they drag their feet past the horses who stand there with garlanded manes.
Some they will see with their heads bowed in a sadness which matches their fortune,
Others will walk in a terrible pride, unmindful of selves.
25 Some of the viewers will ask for their names, their records, their causes,
And others will answer them although they'll know very little to tell:
"This one who shines so grandly in his robe of Phoenician purple,
He was the leader in battle, that one was his next in command.
This one who fixes his eyes now on the earth in his miserable sorrow
30 Did not look at all like this when he carried his weapons of war.
That fierce one whose eyes even now are blazing with hostile emotions
Was once the man who planned battles and urged on his men to the fight.
This treacherous fellow designed an ambush that trapped our battalions,
The one who conceals his distorted features behind his long hair.
35 That one who follows, they tell us, as a priest often sacrificed humans
Who were captured in war to a god who often refused to accept.
This lake, these mountains, these many forts, these rivers that pass by
As floats were full of fierce slaughter, were filled with the blood of men.

94

Drusus among these regions once earned his surnames in battle
40   And bore them, a worthy offspring whose father was proud of him.
This object so poorly covered with green sedge and broken horn fragments
     Is the Rhine river in person, discolored with his own blood.
Look, there is Germany passing, her hair streaming down all about her;
     She sorrowfully sits at the feet of a leader unbeaten in war
45   And offers her neck, once defiant, to the stroke of the Roman ax-handler
     And wears on the hand which once carried its weapons now Roman chains."
Above all these, Caesar, you will be borne in your triumphal carriage,
     Clothed in your ritual purple before the gaze of your folk,
And wherever you go you'll be greeted by clapping of hands all around you
50   And everywhere over the roadway they will toss flowers at you.
Your brows will be circled with laurel of Phoebus, the soldiers will cry out
     "Io triumphe" and "Io" with loud voices again and again.
At the sound of the shouting and clamor, the applause in their ears set a-ringing,
     Your chariot horses will struggle and rear high up in the air.
55   And then you will seek Rome's high fortress and shrines that favor your prayers
     And to Jove to whom you had vowed it you'll give the laurel he deserves.

Stirred by these actions, I'll see them in the one way I can—with my mind's eye:
     For it has the right to that place even if it's denied to me;
60   Freely through unmeasured countries and over the world it will travel
     To attain the heavens themselves in its rapid progress through space.
It will lead my vision and place my eyes in the middle of Rome there,
     Nor allow them to be deprived of so great a good fortune as this.
And my spirit will find a location from which to see your ivory chariot.
65   Thus I am certain I shall be in Rome for at least a short time.
Nevertheless, the fortunate folk will see real spectacles round them

95

And the Roman throng will be happy together with their great chief.
But I through imagination alone since I'm far away from it
And not with my ears will listen to all the joy that they feel,
70 And scarcely sent far from Latium into a different horizon
Will anyone tell me what's happened although I am eager to know.
If anyone comes he will tell me of triumphs late, long since over:
Nonetheless I'll be happy to listen at whatever time.
That day will come when I shall lay aside my sadness and straightway
The cause of the people will be for me greater than my own cause.

3

You wild bears, big one and smaller, one of you guides Greek sailboats
And the other Sidonian vessels, while both are unwetted by waves.
Since you are placed in position at the top of the Pole you view all things
And do not descend into waters that wash the sunsetting west,
5 And since you encircle the height of heaven in the embracing
Of your orbit it extends beyond and never touches the earth.
Look down, I beg, at the walls where once on a time to his sorrow
Remus, the twin son of Ilia, is reported to have leaped across,
And, turning your shimmering visage, shine down on my mistress for me
10 And tell me whether she thinks of—or does not think of me.

Ay me, why do I question things which are all too apparent?
Why does my hope lie fallen, mingled with anxious dread?
Believe that which is as you wish it, and cease to fear what is stable,
And let your faith become certain concerning a faith that is sure,

15 And that which the flames which are fixed to the Pole are unable to tell you,
    Give to yourself your own answer in a voice that never will lie:
That your wife remembers you and that you're all the world to her truly
    And as much as she's able she keeps your name hugged close to her heart,
That she clings to your features as if you were still living with her now
20   And although you've been taken away from her she loves you—if she lives.
Whenever your sick mind has brooded upon your justified sorrow
    Does gentle sleep go away from your heart filled with memories?
Then do your cares assail you when the bed and my place there beside you
    Trouble you, keep you awake, nor allow me to leave your mind,
25 Do attacks of depression arrive and the night seem long and unending
    And do your weary bones ache as you toss about in the bed?
I have no doubt that these feelings and others like them are occurring
    And your love for me reasserts itself in the signs of your grief;
You are tortured no less than Andromache was when she saw him, her husband,
30   Hector all gory and grimed dragged by Greek chariot wheels.

Yet, for myself, I'm in doubt what prayer I should offer, I cannot
    Say what feeling I'd wish for you to present to me.
Are you sad? I am angry because I am the source of your sorrow.
    You are not? Yet you should be sad, as befits a husbandless wife.
35 But truly lament your loss, my gentlest wife of all spouses,
    Live and endure sad days, clouded because of my ills,
And weep for my fate: there is a sort of pleasure in weeping;
    Sorrow is sated with tears and driven away as they fall.
Ah, would that your weeping were not caused by my life, that you could still
40   Weep for my death, that you might by my death be left all alone!
This spirit of mine would have passed by your aid to the air of its homeland

97

And your loving tears would have scattered their moisture upon my breast,
    And on my last day as I stared with fixed gaze at the sky I have known well
        Your fingers would have drawn their lids down over my eyes in death,
45   And my ashes might have been laid to rest in my ancestral graveyard
        While the earth my body had touched when I was born would hold my corpse;
    At last in the way I have lived I would have died—not as a criminal:
        Now my life is ashamed by the form of its punishment.

    I feel like a wretch if you, when you're called the wife of an exile
50   Turn your eyes to one side while a blush ascends in your cheeks!
    I feel like a wretch if you think it a shame to be known as my wife, dear,
        I feel like a wretch if now you are ashamed to be mine!
    Where is the time when you were accustomed to boast you were married
        To me, when you did not try to conceal the name of your man?
55   Where is the time when you—unless you don't wish any mention
        Of it—when it was a joy to be called, and recalled, as mine?
    As befitted a proper wife, I pleased you with every endowment
        Of mine—and to those which were real your love added more of its own.
    There was no one you preferred—so important a man I seemed to you—
60   There was no other husband you would have chosen but me.

    Now also be not ashamed that to me you are married, my dear wife;
        You should be sad at the thought, you should not feel any shame.
    When reckless Capaneus toppled, struck by a thunderbolt's power,
        You have not read that Evadne blushed for her husband, have you?
65   Nor because the king of the world subdued the sun's fire with fire
        Was Phaethon therefore disowned and denied by those who were his friends.

Semele did not become estranged from Cadmus her husband, who loved her,
  Because of the ambitious vows that brought her destruction instead.
Then on your face do not now, because I've been stricken by Jove's hand,
70   Let the red blush of shame spread over its tender skin.
But rather rise to my care and defence, no, rather become now
  The shining example of what it means to be a good wife.
Rise to the occasion, fulfill it with all of your eminent virtues:
  Glory goes up on a path that is headlong and perilous.
75 Who would have known about Hector, if Troy had remained out of danger?
  The way for a hero is paved with many a public ill.
Tiphys, your skill would be idle if there were no waves on the ocean:
  If men were healthy your art, Apollo, we would not need.
Outstanding qualities lie undiscerned while everything goes well;
80   Virtue appears and is known when everything goes dead wrong.
My misfortune gives you the chance to win fame, your loyal love has
  A space in which it can raise its head to the very skies.
Make use of opportunity as it offers a gift you should seize on
  While it opens a place that is broad in which your praises may rise.

4

O you who are noble by means of the names of those who precede you
  Surpass in the nobility of your character your entire clan.
In your spirit there is an image of your father's integral virtue,
  Not that your own luster lacks any splendor that belongs to itself,
5 You who possess the same talent your father had in public speaking,

Where none in the Roman forum had greater skill than he.
I did not wish to describe you by name but in general phrases
    And yet I have named you: forgive me for praises which are all your own.
I have done nothing that's wrong; your virtues are known and betray you.
10   If you appear what you are, I am absolved of all blame.

Nonetheless I do not believe the respect which I pay you in poems
    Can possibly harm you with so fair-minded a leader as ours.
The father of our fatherland—for who is more civil than he is?—
    Allows his name to be read often in poems that are mine;
15 Nor can he prevent it, because the republic is Caesar himself and
    In what is good for the people I too have my own share.
Jupiter offers his powers as a theme for poets to write of
    And permits himself to be praised by whatever lips may wish.
Your cause is defended by the example of two gods above us,
20   One of them visible clearly, the other believed in as god.
Although I need not and should not I'll receive this blame to myself;
    It was not due to your judgment that my letter was written to you.

This is no new offense I commit when I speak with you freely
    For when I was whole and unharmed I often spoke with you.
25 And so that you may not fear lest my friendship to you prove a hazard
    If ill will should arise toward you I take the blame for it.
For from my very first years a man who was honored by my faith—
    This certainly do not attempt to suppress—that man was your father.
He used to praise my talent, as you, I am sure, can remember,
30   More even than I deserved as far as I'm able to judge.

And concerning my poems he was used to express himself in those accents
  Wherein he revealed a large part of his nobility.
Not you therefore now, if this house has received me hospitably,
  Have been deceived but your father was the one cheated before.

35 Your father was never deceived, believe me, in all of my exploits;
  If you omit the last, my life is beyond reproach.
This fault also by which I perished you'd say was no criminal action
  If the chain of events which led to my ills were known well to you.
Either my fear or an error, rather an error brought ruin.
40   Ah, permit me to leave my misfortune unrecalled!
Let me not open by groping among them the wounds which were healing:
  Scarcely will peace and quiet cause them to close once more.
Therefore although with justice I pay the penalty, not one
  Of my deeds or plans had among them the slightest hint of a sin.
45 And this is known to the god, wherefore my life was not taken
  Nor does another possess my property snatched from me.
Perhaps this very exile, if only I live, he will bring me
  One day to an end when his anger has been soothed with the passage of time.

Now I am begging that he should order me to leave this region
50   For some other place, if my prayers do not lack respectful modesty.
I am seeking an exile more gentle and somewhat nearer to Roma,
  A place which would be much farther from the savage enemy here.
So great is Augustus' mercy, if anyone else should request him
  To grant me this favor perhaps he would give it to me.
55 The frigid shores of the Pontic Euxine keep me bound in this region;

It was once named by the ancients Axenus, "inhospitable,"
Because its waters were never ruffled by moderate breezes
    Nor did any foreign vessel cast anchor in its quiet ports.
The tribes that live round about here seek out their booty with carnage
60   Nor is the untrustworthy mainland less feared than the treacherous sea.
Those men whom you've heard rejoice in shedding the blood of poor humans
    Inhabit lands almost beneath the same star under which I live,
And not far from us lies that place where the Taurian altar is standing
    Which is sprinkled with gore from dread slaughter by quivered Diana the queen.

65   Here in old times, as they tell us, lay the realm of Thoas the monarch,
    Not envied by those who were wicked nor desired by those who were good.
Here the Pelopian maiden whom the she-deer replaced in the story
    Cared for the gifts to her goddess, whatever they might have been.
Hither there came Orestes, whether a good man or bad man,
70   After he fled from his Furies, driven away from his home,
And here came his Phocian comrade, the model of truthful affection,
    These men who lived in two bodies but men with a single heart.
Straightway when cast into bonds they were led to the altar so dreadful
    Which stood there dripping with blood in front of twin folds of a door.
75   Yet neither one nor the other was fearful of his own destruction
    But each of them sorrowed because the other was destined to die.
And now the priestess had taken her stand with drawn sword in hand grasp,
    And had bound her Greek hair with a headband made in a barbarous style,
When she spoke with him she recognized her brother and straightway
80   Iphigenia embraced him instead of taking his life.
Joyfully she transported the goddess' statue, who loathed the
    Cruel sacrifice of a human, from there to a better place.

This therefore is the region, almost at the end of the world, one
    Which both men and gods have fled from but which is close to me;
Near to my land they follow the rites of sad sacrifices,
    If a barbarous land near to Naso can really be said to be his.
O would that the winds by whose blowing Orestes was borne from this region
    Might carry my sails and me homeward when a god has been mollified.

5

O you most dearly beloved, most cherished one of my comrades,
    You were the unique altar my fortunes could find for themselves,
Whose comforting words revived this moribund soul in my bosom
    As the vigilant flame is accustomed to revive with the pouring of oil;
5   You who were not afraid to open a welcoming port to my coming
    As a haven for my boat when she was struck by a lightning bolt,
By whose wealth I should have found myself relieved from poverty's need
    If Caesar had seized on the fortune which was left me when my father died:
While in my enthusiasm I forgot both time and occasion
10   I very nearly let slip, to my sorrow, the name that you bear!

But you recognize this fact and, touched by desire for praises,
    You may wish you were able more frankly to say to me "I am that man."
Certainly, if you allowed it, I'd like to do honor to you now
    And to tell in my praises how loyal you are as I utter your fame.
15   But I fear lest a poem to please you might bring harm to you, and I'm fearful
    Lest to name you in awkward season might prove a dishonor instead.
One thing you can do and in safety: rejoice within your own bosom

That I have been mindful of you and that you have been loyal to me,
And as you are doing, bend downwards on your oars to bring me assistance
20   Until there shall start up a gentler breeze from a pacified god,
And rescue a life that no one can save except for the person
        Who caused it to sink underneath the waves of the Stygian stream,
And surrender yourself—what a rare thing!—constantly to every aspect
        Of service and duty that spring from a friendship that never will change.

25 In this way your fortune will fare well with frequent additions of wealth and
        Thus you will stand in no need but be able to help your own,
Thus shall your wife equal her husband in righteousness also
        And quarrels disturb very rarely the peaceful marriage you share.
And may your blood brother continue to love you as he has done thus far
30   With such love as his loyal brother, Pollux, gave Castor as well;
And may your young son who is like you, whenever he's born, be a scion
        Whom all people may discover is yours by the way he behaves.
And thus may the wedding torch lit for your daughter make you a father-
        In-law and soon give the name of a young grandfather to you.

6

In time the long-suffering bullock grows used to the farmer's plowshare
        And bends his neck to be pressed by the weight of the curving yoke;
In time the spirited horse bows his head to the flexible bridle
        And receives with a mouth that is docile the teeth of the roweling bit;
5   In time the wrath of Phoenician lions is pacified wholly
        Nor does there remain as there once was that spirit and fierceness they had;

Each Indian elephant-creature obeys its driver's direction
     And in time it is conquered and bends to its labor of servitude.
Time makes the grapes swell riper as their clusters grow in the vineyard
10   Until each grape scarcely contains the juice that it harbors within.
Time and the seed produce the white ears of the ripening grain field
     And time takes care that the apples do not taste bitter or sour.
Time thins the edge of the plowshare as it cuts and renews the farmland;
     Time wears away rigid flintstones and adamant, hardest of things.
15 It gradually softens men's anger no matter how savage it may be;
     It lessens our sorrows and lifts up the hearts of those who feel low.
Everything therefore the passing of time with its silent footstep
     Can diminish and weaken, yes, everything but my trouble and care.

Since I lost my fatherland, twice the grain on the floor where they thresh it
20   Has been trodden and twice beneath the naked foot the grapes have been pressed.
And yet I have not found patience throughout a long space of time passing,
     And my heart feels its recent misfortune as much as it ever has felt.
Of course, even old bullocks shun the cruel yoke once in a while still
     And the horse that's been tamed nonetheless still bucks at the rein and the bit.
25 My present despair is still harsher than that which I suffered before this:
     For though it's the same it's grown deeper, enlarged with the passage of time.
Nor were the ills that were mine as well known to me then as they are
     Now, and the more that I know them the heavier they are to bear.
It is an advantage as well to bring earlier strength to my sorrows
30   And not to have faced them exhausted by ills that arrive in their time.
There in the yellow arena a fresh fighter's very much stronger
     Than a man whose arm muscles are tired by fighting again and again.
A sound gladiator is better, who bestrides in his shining armor

The sand than one who has crimsoned his enemy's weapons with blood.
35 A vessel of recent construction bears well the precipitate tempest;
An old ship will rapidly founder in a rainstorm no matter how small.
Now too I can scarcely endure what I bore with more patience before this,
My misfortunes which time as it passes has doubled, redoubled again.

I tell you, believe me, I'm failing, as much as I guess from the state of
40 My body; a short time awaits me before I am free of my ills.
For I don't have the strength which I once had nor the color that made my cheeks freshen;
I scarcely have skin which may cover the bones that emerge and stick out.
But my mind is more sick than my body is sick and it broods on its fortunes,
As it endlessly contemplates suffering which seems to abide without end.
45 The sight of the City is missing, the City I loved and my comrades,
And she, than whom nothing is dearer, my wife is far distant from me.
There's a crowd here of Scythian people and a mob of the trousered Getae:
And thus what I see and I don't see both have their effect upon me.
One hope nonetheless there is still here which comforts me caught in this crisis:
50 These evils will not be long lasting because they will end with my death.

7

Twice has the sun come round to me when the chills of the winter have vanished
And twice has completed his journey, touching the Fish as it passed.
Why hasn't your right hand bestirred itself in such a long time now
By writing some lines to "yours truly," however few they might be?
5 Why has your loyalty languished while they wrote letters who were friends
Of much more slight an acquaintance than yours ever has been to me?

Why, as often as I broke the seal of a letter that came here
    Have I hoped I should read at the bottom the letters that spell out your name?
Gods grant that your right hand has often written a letter sent to me
10   But that out of the many you've written the postman has brought none to me.

That my wishes are true is apparent; I'd sooner believe that the visage
    Of Medusa the Gorgon is covered with hair made of dangling snakes,
That there is a girl named Chimaera to whose lower parts dogs are attached and
    Who is made of a lioness parted from a grim serpent by flames,
15 That there are four-footed creatures joined chest to chest with a human,
    That there is a man who is threefold and a dog that is threefold as well,
That there are a Sphinx and the Harpies and Giants with feet that are serpents,
    And a hundred-handed called Gyas and a man who is half man, half bull.

All of these things I'd believe in before I'd believe, my dear fellow,
20   That you've changed in your attitude toward me and abandoned your friendship for me.
There are numberless mountains between me and you and numberless roadways
    And rivers and fields and great many bays of the sea lie between.
There may be one thousand reasons why letters you wrote with your own hand
    And sent them to me have but rarely ever arrived in my hands.
25 But conquer these one thousand reasons and write as often as you can
    So that I shall not always be forced to excuse you to myself, my friend.

8

Already my temples are changing to imitate swans with their plumage:
    This white hair of old age is bleaching the rest of my hair that was black.

Now fragile years come upon me and an age that is helpless and feeble,
    And now in my weakness I scarcely can bear up my body and move.

5   Now is the time when I ought to set an end to the labors of living
    And to live with a heart that's untroubled by fears and reflections of dread,
And those hours of ease that were always the pleasantest thing to my thinking
    To enjoy and at rest to delight myself in the studies I knew,
And to devote myself to my little home and the gods of my household
10   And the fields that were left me by father, the fields that will see him no more,
And upon the breast of my mistress and among my very dear comrades
    To grow old safe and sound in my country, the fatherland where I was born.
Once on a time, in this manner, my youth hoped that this dream would come true,
    That thus I was worthy of passing my years till they came to an end.

15   This is not what the gods decided who over the land and the ocean
    Have driven me far and brought me to the place where Sarmatians live.
Battered ships are hauled up into dry dock, where they are both built and repaired
    Lest without any need they break up in the midst of the turbulent sea.
So that he won't fall and in falling dishonor his ribbons of triumph
20   The tired-out race horse is cropping the grass in the meadows at home.
When a soldier is no longer useful and his years of retirement come on
    He lays down as gifts to the Lares the weapons he carried to war.
Thus also when old age that slows one down and diminishes power
    Has arrived I should also be given the veteran's sword made of wood.
25   It's time for me not to be breathing the air in a foreign climate
    Nor quenching my thirst in the waters where Getic springs bubble up
But now to retreat to the gardens once mine and to sit in their shadows
    And now to enjoy myself seeing my friends in the City again.

108

Thus in my heart once, divining nothing of what comes in the future,
30   I hoped to be able to live out my years, a placid old man.
The Fates were against me, who gave me a youth that was graced with full leisure
        In my earlier years, but the later they made heavy with my distress,
And now that ten lusters or fifty years of my life have been ended
        Unblemished, I'm crushed in the harder and worst of my later years.
35   Not far from the pillars that mark the goal—I had almost arrived there—
        My chariot wheels have gone crashing and knocked me out of the race.
Did I therefore compel him in my madness to rage against me,
        Than whom the wide world wherever holds no one more gentle than he,
Has that mercy of his been conquered by all of my sins and my failings,
40   And yet in repayment of error my life has not been denied,
A life I must spend far from my country beneath the North Pole in the heavens
        In a land that lies to the left-hand as you enter the Euxine Sea?

If the oracle of Dodona or Delphi should give me this answer
        Both shrines would have seemed unworthy to be believed by me.
45   Nothing is quite so sturdy, although reinforced with steel rivets,
        To withstand more firmly the fire and shock of Jupiter's bolt;
Nothing there is so lofty that extends beyond perils above us
        That is not placed on a level subjected beneath a god.
For although by my sin I drew part of my ills upon my own shoulders
50   Yet the wrath of divinity's power has given me more misery.

But you who read be admonished by what has happened in my case
        To make yourselves worthy of favor from a man who is equal to gods.

9

If I may and if you allow it, I'll keep silent your name and your misdeed,
  And what you have done shall be given to Lethe's forgetful waves,
My judgment shall be refuted by the late tears you have scattered
  If only you show your repentance sincerely and clearly to me,
5 If only you curse your actions and wish to erase from your record
  Those damnable days of the Furies you spent committing your crimes.

If not, and your heart is still burning with hatred directed at myself,
  Unhappy and full of my sorrows I'll be forced to take arms against you.
Although I be sent, just as I am, to ends of the earth that are farthest
10   My anger shall stretch and its weapons even as far as you are.
All of my rights, if you don't know, great Caesar has left me completely,
  And my only penalty-payment is the lack of my fatherland.
And yet I can hope to regain it from him while he is still living:
  Often the oak tree that's blasted by Jupiter's lightning still lives.

15 Furthermore, if there's no chance of real vengeance that I can accomplish
  The Pierian Muses have power and they'll give their weapons to me.
Although I dwell far from my homeland thrust out upon Scythian sea shores
  And the Zodiac signs which are dry are the ones which are close to my eyes
Yet my clarion call will go crying through numberless nations and earth-wide
20   And my accusations wherever the world stretches out shall be heard.
Whatever I say shall go flying from sunrise to where the sun settles
  And the East shall be witness to my voice which rises from out of the West.

Across the land I shall be heard, I'll be heard across the deep waters,
　　And the sound of my voice in its howling shall be exceedingly great.
25　Not only your generation shall know you're a consummate scoundrel
　　But your crime will be known to the people who will form your posterity.

Now, now I am borne into battle though not yet have I taken up weapons
　　And I'd wish there were not any reason why I ever should take them up.
The circus games have not started; already the glowering bull there
30　　Is scattering sand and stamping the ground with his dangerous hoof.
This too is more than I wished for; Muse, sound retreat on your bugle,
　　As long as this man is allowed to conceal the name which he bears.

10

I am that man who has been the gay poet of tender lovemaking,
　　The man whom you read, accept me, posterity, so that you may know.
The place of my birth was at Sulmo, most rich with its cooling streamlets;
　　It lies at a distance from Rome which amounts to just ninety miles.
5　And so that you may know in addition the exact time when I was born,
　　It was the year when both consuls succumbed to a similar fate.
If this is worth saying, I was the heir of men of ancient standing,
　　Not one made a knight by good fortune that recently fell to my lot.
Nor was I the first of the children; my brother was older than I was.
10　　He came ahead of me since he was born twelve months before me.
The same Morning Star was above us when each of us came into being.

Our birthday was celebrated by two birthday cakes, one for each.
This is that day among five days when Minerva the weaponed the first time
    Is stained with the blood of the combats that are offered in worship to her.

15 We were educated since we were little; our father was careful to send us
    To Rome, there to be instructed by men trained in liberal arts.
My brother went in for public speaking while he was still youthful,
    Born for the wordy forum and its brave clashing of arms.
But for me while I was still a stripling the heavenly rites were my pleasure
20   And little by little, discreetly, the Muse drew me into her arts.
Often my father told me: "Why this useless endeavor?
    Homer himself left nothing behind him of worldly wealth."
I was influenced by his warning and I left mount Helicon flatly,
    And I tried to write prose that was free from the rhythms of poetry's style.
25 Yet all by themselves the rhythms of poetry came to me smoothly,
    And what I attempted to write was—well, you can guess: it was verse.

Meanwhile in its silent passing down through the gliding seasons
    Time brought the toga of manhood to both my brother and me.
And we slung on our shoulders a garment marked by a broad stripe of purple
30   While our pursuits and desires remained what they were before.
And now my brother had doubled ten years in all of his lifetime
    When he died, and I began missing the better part of myself.
I took on the first position granted to my tender age group
    And I became part of and served on a board made up of three men.
35 The Senate awaited, but I cut my stripe to a narrower border:
    That burden of power was greater than my strength could arise to assume.

112

My body had not the endurance nor my mind was fit for the function,
    And I was a fugitive from the anxious political life.
The Aonian sister-Muses kept urging me toward what was safer,
40   The leisurely arts and diversions which always appealed to my mind.

I cherished and cultivated the poets who lived at that moment,
    And whatever bards were around me I thought of as so many gods.
Often Macer would read me, a man who was older than I was,
    His poems on birds, and on serpents that kill, and on herbs that preserve.
45 Often Propertius read me his poems full of fire and loving
    By right of that comradeship joining us one another to each.
Ponticus famed in the epic and Bassus the same in iambic
    Were also beloved members of the circle of poets I knew.
Horace of many rhythms was one who held my ears captive
50   While he struck on his lyre the polished strains of Italian song.
Vergil—I merely saw him, nor did stingy death in its passing
    Give me the time to become a friend to Tibullus himself.
He was your successor, Gallus, and Propertius followed Tibullus;
    I was the fourth among these, both in the series and time.

55 And just as I cherished my elders the younger men made me their hero,
    And my Muse, who is Thalia, prospered early on in my career.
At the time when I first read my youthful poems in public I had yet
    Cut off my beard with a razor not more than one or two times.
The woman who stirred into action my talent was sung throughout Roma;
60   In my verses I used not her real name; she was called Corinna by me.

I wrote many poems at any rate but those I thought worthless
    With my own hands I burned in the fire, a final revision in flames.
At the time of my flight I burned also some poems readers might have liked
    Because I was angry with writing, with talent, with all of my poems.

65   I was weak and soft and my heart was not storm-proof against Cupid's arrows,
    A heart that was stirred by the slightest attack of an amorous sort.
However, although I was like this, set on fire by sparks that are smallest,
    My name never figured in scandal nor gossip of any kind.
When still a boy my parents gave me a wife quite unworthy;
70   We were married but we lived together for only a very brief time.
Her successor, although as long as she was my wife she was blameless,
    Was destined however to grace our marriage bed briefly as well.
The last wife I have has lived with me down into my later lifetime
    And she has endured to be wife to a man who is exiled from home.
75   My daughter, who had become pregnant twice in her first years of marriage
    But not by one husband has made me a grandfather, I'm proud to say.
And now my father had filled out his fate and had added to his age
    Nine lusters of years together with another nine—hence ninety years.
I wept for him just as he would have wept for me if I were dead.
80   He died; and next I brought mother the final offerings of death.
Both of them happy and both of them buried just at the right time
    Because they perished before the day when my punishment came!
I too am happy because they were not alive at the moment
    When I became wretched and because they did not sorrow for me!
85   If nevertheless there is something beyond names that remains from the dead folk,
    If a tenuous shadow escapes the pyres erected for them,

If the shame of my reputation, parental shades, has arrived there
      Among you and my transgression is known in the Stygian realm,
Know then, I pray you, the cause (for it isn't right to deceive you).
90   An error it was that made me an exile, it wasn't a crime.

Thus much for the shades of the dead: to you, my studious readers,
      I return, to answer your questions about the events of my life.
Now my gray hairs when my best years fled with those years that were better
      Have come upon me and been mixed with the rest of my ancient locks.
95 After my birth the race horse crowned with olive had triumphed
      And ten times carried as victor the prize of the races away
When the wrath of an injured ruler bade me to seek the environs
      Of Tomis lying upon the left hand of the Euxine Sea.
The cause of my ruin is also too well known now to all people
100   And needs no testification at this late date from me.
What shall I say of disloyal friends, of the harm my slaves have done me?
      Much did I suffer before I left that's more grievous than flight.
My spirit refused to give in to my misfortunes and stood up
      Unconquered against such destruction, relying upon its own strength,
105 And forgetting myself and the life I had led in the pathways of leisure
      I took up in hand unaccustomed arms which the times had supplied,
And on land and on sea I suffered so many sorrows as the stars
      That appear in the sky between the hidden and visible poles.

Driven through many long wanderings at last I touched on the seashores
110   Which link the Sarmatian people, who wear quivers, with the Getes.
Here although I'm surrounded by the sound of my neighbors in battle

115

The sad fate I suffer I lighten in what way I can, with song.
Although there is no one about me to whose ears I can utter my poems
In this way at least I beguile and wear out the time of the day.

115 Therefore because I continue to live and resist my harsh fortunes
And a complete disgust for this worrisome life does not depress me
I am grateful, my Muse, to you because you offer me solace,
Rest and release from care, medicine for my veins.
You are my leader and comrade, you draw me away from the Danube,
120 You give me a place in the midst of Helicon hill on its top.
You have given me something that's rare, an illustrious name in my lifetime,
Something that fame is accustomed to give only when you are dead.
Nor has Jealousy, which detracts the present, with its teeth malignant
Gnawed at any one work among the books that are mine.
125 And although my age has produced great men who are excellent poets
Fame has never denied its graceful self to my works.
And although I place many others above me, not less than they are
I have been called, and I am read most in the entire world.
If therefore the vaticinations of bards have a bit of truth in them
130 Immediately after I'm dead I shall not be yours, O earth.
Whether I've garnered this fame through favor or by means of my poems
With justice I render my thanks, my candid reader, to you.

BOOK V

1

This book as well, my reader, who zealously cherish my poems,
　　To the four I have sent you already from the shores of the Getae, add this.
This book will also resemble the fate which the poet complains of;
　　You will find in its entire contents not a single line that is sweet.
5　Just as my condition is tearful, so tearful will be my poems;
　　The rhythm and flow of the writing are in harmony with their theme.
When I was sound-limbed, in fine fettle, I wrote jolly juvenile poems;
　　Now I'm ashamed that I ever sat down and wrote them at all.
Since I fell I broadcast the clarion call of my sudden dismissal,
10　And I am myself the creator of a story about my sad self.
As the swan lies moaning upon the river bank of Cayster
　　And is said to mourn for its death with a faintly diminishing song
Thus I, prostrate on the shores of Sarmatia far in the distance,
　　Take care that my funeral rites are not ignored, without even a sound.

15 If anyone looks for delightful and slightly pornographic verses,
    I'm warning him, this isn't written for a man of his kind to read.
    Gallus is more to his liking and Propertius with his hot, sweet lips,
        And Tibullus will suit him more fully, sophisticate, charming, and gay.
    And I would that I had not been reckoned among the number of these men!
20   Ay me, why ever did my Muse make sport in my poems at all?
    But I've paid the penalty for it; to the lands of Scythian Danube
        That fellow who sported with Amor, who wears a quiver, is gone.
    In the time that is left me I've turned my lines into "Poems for All People"
        And bidden my public to keep in their minds the words of this name.

25 However, if there is someone among you who asks me the question
        Why I sing about so many sorrows it's because I have suffered them all.
    I haven't just made up a story employing my art and my talent;
        The contents I use for my poems correspond to my personal ills.
    And how small a part of my fortunes is included here in my poems?
30   Happy the man who can reckon the misfortunes he's forced to bear!
    As many as shrubs in the forest or the yellow sands of the Tiber,
        As many as tender grass blades which grow green in the Field of Mars,
    So many evils I've suffered for which there's no cure and no surcease
        Except in the poetic passion I feel as I serve my Muse.
35 "What limit is there to your tearful poem, Naso?" you ask me:
        The very same limit there is to the wearisome life which I live.
    The sources for my lamentation arise from a bountiful fountain,
        These are not my words which I'm writing, they are the accents of fate.

    But if you should give back my dear wife and give back my fatherland
40   My face would resume its happy look, I'd become what I was.
    If the anger of unconquered Caesar should grow less severe toward me

118

I should write poetry for you that is filled with nothing but joy.
Yet never again will my verses make sport as they did when I wrote them:
Let them but once and once only find mischievous joy in my ill!
45 I shall write poems he'll approve of if only a partial assuagement
Of my punishment comes and escape from these barbarians known as the Getes.
In the meanwhile what else shall my books say except how sorrowful I am?
These are the flutes that should sound at my funeral service today.

"But you could," you say, "bear your sorrow more easily by keeping quiet
50 And in silence pretend that your troubles have never happened at all."
Do you ask me that I should not groan when the torturer twists his engine?
And when I've been wounded severely, you tell me that I shouldn't cry?
Phalaris gave to Perillus permission to howl in the brazen
Statue he made and to bellow out of the mouth of the bull.
55 When the weeping of Priam did not provoke the Greek hero Achilles
Would you check my tears and behave more harshly than an enemy?
When the children of Leto deprived Niobe of sons and of daughters
They did not order that she should hold back the tears from her cheeks.
It's something at least to relieve the evils of fate with one's language:
60 This is what caused Halcyone and Procne to utter their grief.
This is why sad Philoctetes there in his lone chilly cavern
Wearied the rocks of the island of Lemnos with his laments.
A grief that is checked simply chokes us, seething and boiling within us,
And is forced in its straitened location to multiply all of its strength.
65 Rather give me your indulgence or take away all of my writings
If that which is useful to me, my reader, is harmful to you.
Yet my poetry writings cannot do any harm to anyone else for
They have done damage to none except to their author alone.

119

"But they're poor poems." I grant you: who compels you to take up bad poems?
70   Or who forbids you to lay them aside when you find that you've been deceived?
Even I do not correct them, but let them be read here as written;
    They are not more barbarous than the barbarous place where they grew.
Rome would not compare me to poets who live there because of this reason:
    It's among the Sarmatian people that I was a talented man.

75 Finally, I'm not ambitious for fame or any great glory
    Of the kind that's accustomed to spur poetical talents like mine.
I do not wish that my soul should pine with continual sorrows
    Which nevertheless break in on me, intruding where they are denied.

The reason I write I have told you; why do I send you my poems,
80   You ask? Because I desire to be with you in what way I can.

2

Whenever a new letter comes out of Pontus, do you shrink and turn pallid
    And open it up with a hand which trembles with worry and fear?
Do not be frightened, I'm healthy; my body which when I was younger
    Could not bear stresses or labors and was almost useless to me
5 Is strong now; at least it's sufficient to stand the life it must bear with,
    Or is it rather that I have no time nor the wish to be weak?

My mind, however, is sickly nor does it grow stronger with aging.
    That same depression of spirit which it suffered before it has now.

And the wounds which I thought with the passing of time would close up in healing
10   Are paining me still just as if they were inflicted on me yesterday.
Of course, time full of the rolling years can assist in small evils;
    In great troubles time only adds to the damage they've already done.
Philoctetes nourished for almost ten years on his Lemnian island
    The pestiferous wound which was given him by the swollen snake;
15 Telephus would have expired, consumed by his long-standing illness,
    Had not the hand which had wounded him also provided its aid.

And my wounds, if I have committed no crime, I am fervently hopeful
    That he who inflicted them may wish to relieve them once they were made,
And contented at last with a small part of the suffering inflicted upon me
20   He should draw off a bit of the water out of a plentiful sea.
Although he should draw off a large part, a large part will still remain always
    Of my bitterness; part of my penalty will resemble the whole.
As many as shells on the seashore, or as roses that grow in the garden,
    Or as many as seeds of the poppy that puts anybody to sleep,
25 As many beasts as the forest feeds, or the fish in the ocean,
    Or as many the feathers with which a bird beats the yielding air,
By so many troubles I'm crushed; if I tried to include them completely,
    Just as well I should try to count up the drops in the Icarian Sea,
To say nothing of dangers of travel, harsh perils suffered on shipboard,
30   Or from many hands that were lifted to kill me as I journeyed here,
I live in a barbarous country at the uttermost end of the wide world
    In a place ringed around and begirdled by the most savage enemies.

From here I might have been rescued—for my fault's not one that is bloody
    If you had exerted your efforts for me as you should have done.

121

35 That god upon whom Roman power is based in the happiest manner
        Was often a gentle victor who treated his enemies well.
    Why do you hesitate, fearing what's safe? Approach and implore him:
        Than Caesar there's nothing more gentle in the whole wide world where we live.
    I'm wretched! What shall I be doing when deserted by nearest and dearest?
40   Do you also draw out your neck like an ox from its broken yoke?
    Where shall I be borne? Whence shall I seek solace in my sad condition?
        There is no anchor which now any longer restrains my boat.
    He shall see to it himself; to the sacred altar, though I am
        Hated, I'll run, for an altar never thrusts off human hands.

45 Look, as a distant suppliant to the distant powers I'll pray then
        If it is allowed to a mortal to be able to speak with Jove:

    Lord of the Empire, so long as you're safe the race of Ausonia
        Possesses assurance that it has care and protection from gods;
    O you, the honor and image of a fatherland prosperous through you,
50   O hero not less great than the very world over which you rule—
    Thus may you dwell on the earth and the ether above long to have you.
        Thus may you go but be late in your going to promised stars—
    Spare me, I beg you, and from your lightning withdraw the least part;
        That which remains will be for me a penalty quite large enough.

55 Your anger indeed's not excessive, for you have spared my existence
        Nor have you taken my right of a citizen or its name away.
    Nor has my fortune been granted to other men nor am I listed
        By the terms of your edict an "exile", and all other rights I retain.
    Of all of these things I am fearful because I deserved them, I grant you,

60 But your anger has proved to be gentler than the sin which called it to life:
    You have ordered me as "relegated" to view the fields of the Pontic
        And to cut the Scythian waters in a boat that flies over the sea.
    As ordered, I came to the Euxine and then to its repellent sea shores
        —This is a land that lies under the chilly Pole of the North—
65 It's not that I'm so tormented by a climate that's always so chilly
        And a soil that is always covered with a coating of white hoar frost,
    And a barbarous tongue that is foreign to sounds of the Latin language,
        And the Greek language that's overcome by the ring of the Getic words
    As the fact that I am surrounded by warfare that's close all about me
70   And the wall that protects me can scarcely keep any enemies out.
    Yet peace there is sometimes but never the feeling that peace is enduring:
        So the place now suffers attack and now fears that attack will come.

    As long as I might leave this region, let Zanclaean Charybdis swallow
        Me in its waters and send me down to the waters of Styx,
75 Or let me in patience be burned in the flames of Aetna's volcano,
        Or be thrown into the deep waters the way that they do in Leucas.
    What I seek is to serve out my sentence, for I do not refuse what is proper
        To a wretch, but I pray to be able to suffer more safely than here.

3

This is that day upon which we who are poets salute you,
    (If I've not mistaken the date), Bacchus, a custom we have,
And to weave round our festive temples garlands of odorous vine leaves
    And to lift our praises on high as we drink the wines you have made.

5 Among them, as I recall, while my fates were still smiling upon me
   I have been often a part not without favor to you,
 I, placed beneath the stars of the Cynosurian she-bear,
   Am detained on the shores of Sarmatia linked to the barbarous Getes,
 And who earlier lived without labors a life full of softness and leisure
10   Devoted to studies of verse and to the Pierian Muse,
 Now I am far from my country, surrounded by Getic weapons,
   I who before had suffered much upon land and on sea.
 Whether misfortune produced my state or the wrath of the high gods
   Or whether when I was a-borning the Fate was covered with clouds,
15 Yet you should have toward one who worships your ivy divine then
   Given him all the support of the power that is yours alone.

 Or whatever the sister Muses, mistresses of fate, have sung out,
   Does it entirely cease to be governed by will of a god?
 You too because of your merits have been carried to heavenly levels
20   And the way to them was accomplished with no small labor by you;
 You did not dwell in your country but all the way to the snowy
   Strymon river you came and the Getae, worshippers of Mars,
 And to Persia and to the Ganges, flowing with streams of wide water,
   And to all of the waters whatever the dark-skinned Indian drinks.
25 Such no doubt was the law which the Parcae, spinning your future,
   Sang for you twice (for you were born by a double birth).

 Upon me as well, if it's right to compare my lot with that of the gods,
   An iron-hard fate bears down and a very difficult life,
 And I have fallen no more lightly than he who was driven
30   From Thebes by Jove's thunderbolt, after he made a proud boast.

124

But since you have heard that a poet was struck by a bolt of lightning
      You might have grieved at his lot, recalling your mother's fate,
And, looking around at the poets beside your altar, have spoken:
      "Someone who renders me worship is missing, whoever he is."

35   Bring me, Bacchus, your aid; thus may there weigh down the elm tree
      A pale white vine and its grape be filled with its pent-up juice;
Thus may the active youth of the Satyrs mingled with Bacchae
      Be present for you and your name ring out with a frenzied sound;
Thus may the bones of Lycurgus, who carries an axe, be well pressed down
40   Nor may the impious shade of Pentheus be free from its pain:
Thus may there shine and surpass the neighboring stars forever
      The beautiful crown of your wife glittering up in the sky:
Come to me here and relieve my fate, most handsome of high gods,
      Keep in your mind that I am one of your devotees.
45   Relations exist between gods; make an attempt to persuade the
      Power of Caesar with that power, Bacchus, that's yours.

You poets also, a group that's loyal and shares in my studies,
      Take up the unmixed wine and each make the self-same plea.
And let someone from your midst, toasting the name of Naso,
50   Lift to his lips the cup filled with the mingled wine,
And, thinking of me while he looks around at his circle of comrades,
      Let him say: "Where's Naso today, who once was a part of our band?"
So let it be if I with my zeal have won your approval
      And no letter of any book is injured by judgment of mine,
55   If while I revere the books of old writers since they are worthy
      The men who are recent I hold of no less value than those,

125

Thus therefore may you write your verse with Apollo in favor,
    And, as is fit and allowed, preserve my name among you.

4

I, a letter of Naso, have come from the shore of the Euxine,
    Made weary by travel upon the water, made weary on land;
My writer said to me, weeping: "See Rome, for to you it's permitted;
    Alas, how much better a lot is the one you possess than is mine!"
5   He also wept when he wrote me nor first to his mouth lifted upward
    The gem which he used as a seal but to his tear-dripping cheeks.

If anyone seeks for the answer to the question why I am grieving
    He is asking for someone to show him the sun that shines in the sky;
He doesn't see leaves in the forest nor soft grass in the open meadow,
10   He doesn't see water that flows down when the river is full.
He will wonder why Priam was stricken with grief when Hector was slaughtered
    Or why Philoctetes kept moaning when he was struck by the snake.
Would that the gods might bring Ovid into such a position where he too
    Would require the cause of his sorrow to be enlightened for him!

15   Nevertheless, as he ought, he bears patiently his bitter fortune,
    Nor rears against reins in the manner of an unbroken horse.
Nor does he expect that the anger of the power will always be baleful
    Who's aware that a fault lay in Ovid, that he had not committed a crime.
He often recalls just how great is the mercy of that god of which he's
20   Accustomed to number himself among the examples displayed:

126

That is, he retains his paternal wealth and his citizen's power,
    And finally that he's alive he counts as a gift of the god.

Nonetheless, you (if in anything you believe me, you're dearer
    To him than all others) he always keeps you deep in his heart;
25   You he calls his Patroclus, you are Pylades for him;
    He calls you his Theseus, he calls you also his Euryalus.
He does not long for his country and the many things which are taken
    Away with his country, while missing so keenly whatever is gone,
More than he longs for your eyes and your face, O sweeter than that sweet
30   Honey, where bees in their Attic waxen combs store it away.

Often as well as he grieves that time he clearly remembers
    Which he regrets was not anticipated by his own death
When others were shunning contagion carried by his sudden downfall
    Nor wished to set foot on the doorsill of a house that was stricken with doom
35   You with a few other persons he recalls stood steadfast and firmly,
    If anyone can call two or three persons correctly "a few."
Although he was stunned nonetheless he felt everything still through his sorrow
    And that you no less than he also experienced pain at his fate.
He is wont to recall what you told him, your face, your lament he remembers
40   And the folds of his toga before him wet with your tears on his breast:
How you gave him support and consoled him, his friend then as you were always
    Although you required his comfort as much as he needed yours.

For all this he declares he'll remember and pledge his loyalty also,
    Whether he looks upon daylight or is covered over with soil,
45   By his very life he takes oath and by yours he's accustomed to swear it,

127

Which I know he holds not more cheaply than he considers his own.
Full thanks he will render for so many and such great deeds you have done him,
Nor will he allow your oxen to plough up an empty shore.
But see that you faithfully care for him as a fugitive; that which
50   He does not ask who well knows you I am now asking instead.

5

The year demands its accustomed birthday feast for my mistress:
    My hands, proceed to perform the sacred rites of my love.
Thus did Odysseus the hero once celebrate his helpmate's birthday
    Perhaps at the very edge of the world as he sailed overseas.
5   Let me have with me a tongue of good omen, forgetting misfortunes,
    Which long ago has unlearned how to speak propitiously;
And the robe that I put on once only each year now let me slip into,
    A garment of white which is unbefitting my sorrowful fate;
And let the altar be made from a piece of grassy green turf-mold
10   And let a garland that's woven veil the smouldering hearth.
Give me incense, my boy, the stuff that fattens the fire
    And the unmixed wine that makes hissing sounds in the sacred flames.

Best of all birthday gods! though I'm far away I am hopeful
    That you may come here in a brightness far different from what is mine,
15   And if any miserable wound is pressing my lady's body
    May she recover forever from it by means of my ills
And may my boat which but recently was all but demolished
    In a storm sail on in the future over a tranquil sea.

128

May she enjoy her home and her daughter, her native country—
20   It is enough that one only has been deprived of them—I—
And inasmuch as she has not been blessed in her darling husband
        May the rest of her life be free from the gloom of this hanging cloud.
May she live, may she love her husband from a distance as she must learn to do
        And live out her years till they end, but let their end come to her late.
25 I should add to hers also my own but I am afraid the infection
        Of my fate may corrupt the years which she is passing herself.
Nothing is certain for humans; could anyone think it would happen
        That I should offer these rites in the midst of the savage Getes?
Yet see how the breeze bears off the smoke of the burning incense
30   Toward the direction where lies Italy and good-omened lands.
Sensation exists therefore in the clouds thrown off by the fire:
        With purpose they fly from the sky which, Pontus, rises above.
With purpose when rites were prepared at the altar in common by those two
        Brothers who died in the end, slain by each other's hand,
35 In discord with its own self as though they had ordered it this way
        The black ash of their rite was split into two different parts.
This, I remember, I said once on a time could not happen
        And in my judgment the son of Battus was completely wrong:
I believe everything now since you, vapor, out of the Arctic
40   Have wisely turned back on the North and now seek Ausonia.

This therefore is the day which if it had never arisen
        There would be no birthday for my miserable eyes to see.
This day gave a character forth which equals that of those ladies
        Whom Eëtion and Icaros fathered—Andromache, Penelope.
45 This day was born chastity, and pure thought and loyalty also,

But this is not the day when the joy of my life was born:
Only weariness, cares, and a fate unfit for your nature
    And complaint that is almost just concerning your widowed couch.

Of course a mind that is upright is tested by adverse conditions,
    And a time which is full of sorrow provides the basis for praise.
If steadfast Odysseus had seen no misfortunes engaged on his journey
    Penelope would have been glad but she would have been without praise.
If her husband the victor had pressed on into Echion's fortress
    Perhaps Evadne would have been scarcely known in her land.
Though Pelias had many daughters why is only one of them famous?
    Surely because she was the one who was wed to a miserable man.
Suppose that another was first to set foot on the sands of the Troad:
    Laodamia would have no reason to be recalled.
And your loyalty, as you prefer, would remain forever unheard of
    If favorable winds for my course should have filled my sails as I fled.

You gods nonetheless and Caesar, to join them sometime in the future,
    When the days of your fate are equal to those of old Nestor, the Greek,
Spare not me who confess that I merit your penalty, spare her,
    A woman who grieves although she does not deserve to grieve.

6

You too who were once my defense, you the bulwark of my fortunes,
    You with whom I took refuge, you my port in a storm,

130

Do you too abandon the charge of a friend who's placed in your protection
    And so swiftly lay down the load of your faith and your duty as well?

5   A burden I am, I admit it, but if you were going to lay me
    Down when my luck goes wrong you should not have taken it up.
In the midst of the waves of the ocean are you jumping ship, Palinurus?
    Do not abandon her lest your faith should be less than your skill!
The faithful Automedon did not give way to a light inclination
10   And in the fierce battle let loose Achilles' fiery steeds.
When once he'd accepted his medical duty never did Podalirius
    Fail to bring to the sick man the healing art he had pledged.
It's worse to thrust out a guest than not to have taken him in first:
    The altar, once opened to me, should be firm beneath my right hand.

15   Nothing except me alone did you first protect; now as ever
    Protect me likewise and thus preserve your own judgment that's sound,
If only there is no new fault to be charged against me and your faith
    Has not been suddenly changed because of the wrongs I have done.
May the breath which I draw not well here in the barbarous Scythian climate,
20   As I desire, depart out of my body before
Your heart should be sickened and hurt by any of my transgressions
    And I should deserve to appear less worthy to you than I am.

Not yet to such an extent am I driven by my evil fortune
    That my mind is also unhinged with its long series of ills.
25   Yet imagine it is unhinged, how many times do you reckon
    That Orestes uttered his curse against his good friend Pylades?
Nor is it far from the truth that he even struck blows at his comrade:

131

The latter, however, remained no less firm in his faith.
This is the only thing held in common by wretched and happy
30   Men, that both are accustomed to be treated with respect.
We give way both to the blind and the young, revered in their togas
    Of childhood, and those whom the rod of authority gives reverence.
If you do not have pity upon me at least you should spare my misfortune:
    There is no place left in me for the anger of anyone else.

35 Seek out the least, very least of the ills that have happened to strike me,
    It will be larger than that which you imagine it to be.
As many as there are wet ditches concealed by the tall reeds that grow there,
    As many as honey bees which flowered mount Hybla protects,
As many as ants which by slender paths to their underground storehouse
    Are wont to carry the kernels of grain they have found in the fields,
So great and in such a large crowd are the evils which stand all around me:
    Believe me, the complaint that I raise is less than the cause which it has.
Who's not content with my words let him pour sands on the seashore,
    Grains of wheat into the field, water drops into the sea.
Therefore restrain your anger which comes at a moment unsuited
    And do not desert my sails here in the midst of the sea.

7

This letter which you are reading comes out of that land to you from
    Where the wide Danube adds his waters to those of the sea.
If it should happen that you are alive and in excellent fettle
    A glowing share of my fortune remains to shine upon me.

5   Of course, you ask me as always, my dearest, how am I faring
        Although you could know this even if I should say nothing at all.
I am wretched; this is the substance and sum of the ills that befall me,
        And so is whoever has injured Caesar and still lives on.

The crowd of the Tomitan people, and what this region's compared to,
10   And among what customs I dwell, would you care to know all about these?
Although on the coast there's a mixture of Getae and Greeks in conjunction
        The greater share of the people descend from unpacified Getes.
A larger horde of Sarmatic and Getic races ride past me,
        Going and coming on horseback, keeping the center of roads.
15 There's not a man among them who doesn't wear bow and a quiver
        And arrows which are dipped in poison, yellow with viper's gall.
Their voices are rough and their faces are fierce, the most true image of Mars,
        Their hair and their beards grow shaggy, uncut by the hand of man.
Their right hands are ready to stab you with a dagger they're eager to handle
20   Which every barbarian carries slung in a belt at his side.

Ah, here he lives now among these, forgetful of playful love poems!
        He looks upon these, my friend, that bard of yours listens to these:
If only he'd live among them and not die among them, to cap all,
        So that his spirit might fly away from the place which he hates.

7B

25 Although you write that my poems are set to a choric arrangement
        For full theater and my verse, my friend, receives hearty applause

I have not written—you know this yourself—anything called a drama,
    Nor is my Muse one who craves to hear the clapping of hands.
Not that I am ungrateful for whatever prevents my poems
30   From being forgotten and brings back an exile's name to men's lips,
Although sometimes I remember the poems which injured my status
    And then I curse both the poems and the Muses who gave them to me;
And yet when I've thoroughly cursed them I cannot exist without them
    And I seek for my wounds the bloody weapons that gave them rise,
35 And a Grecian ship which but lately was shaken by Euboean waters
    Still dares to sail over the waves that roll around Cape Caphareus.

And yet I do not keep vigil to be praised for a name that's immortal
    Nor write to preserve what might have more usefully been concealed.
I beguile my mind with my studies and entice my sorrows to leave me.
40   I busy my wits with the purpose of trying to cheat my cares.
What else should I do, deserted, alone upon desolate seashores,
    What other resource should I seek for the evils which fall to my lot?

Whether I look at surroundings, they are revolting, and there is
    Nothing that's sadder to look at anywhere in the wide world,
45 Or at the men who are scarcely worthy the name of humans,
    They are more cruel and savage than even the wolves that roam.
They do not fear laws but justice yields to brute force in their customs
    And the rights that are common to mankind fall under their quarrelsome swords.
With skins and loose-hanging breeches they keep off the evil chill winter
50   And their faces are shaggily covered with locks of stringy long hair.
Few of them keep the traces of the Greek tongue which once they had babbled
    And even these are distorted with the accent of barbarous words.

There isn't a single human among this people I've found yet
    Who can summon by chance the Latin to say the simplest of things.

55   I am a Roman poet—forgive me, my Muses, forgive me—
    And I am forced to say many things in Sarmatian speech.
I am ashamed, I admit it, that through a long lapse of time's passing
    The words of my Latin language scarcely come into my mind.
I have no doubt that in even this book there are more than a handful
60   Of barbarian words; they are not the fault of the man but this place.
Yet just to prevent my losing the use of the Latin language
    Lest my voice be made dumb and unable to utter its native sounds,
I talk to myself and I handle words that are long unfamiliar
    And seek once again the sinister symbols that form my art.
65   Thus I busy my spirit, drag out the time, and withdraw my
    Senses from contemplation of the state of misfortune I'm in.
I seek with my poems oblivion of all my wretched condition:
    If I can win this reward by my zeal, it will be enough.

8

I have not fallen so far, although I am sunken, that I should
    Stand below you, than whom there's nothing lower at all.
What stirs your anger against me, you scoundrel? or what is the reason
    You hurl insults at my fate, which you yourself could suffer now?
5   Don't my ills as I lie there make you mild and more peaceful,
    Such misfortunes as might make even the wild beasts weep?
Don't you fear the power of Fortune who stands on a globe that is slippery,

She who's the goddess that hates all the proud words of men?
But Nemesis, she who avenges, exacts her due expiation:
10   Why with your foot placed upon me do you tread down my fate?
I've seen a man drowned in the sea who had earlier laughed at a shipwreck,
       And "Never," I said "were the waves more just in their punishment."
A man who had once refused to give cheap food to the needy
       Now feeds himself on the food he finds as a beggar man.
15 Fortune, who turns as she goes, wanders with steps that are aimless,
       Abiding in no fixed place, constant in none of her haunts.
Now she beams gayly at us, now puts on a somber deportment,
       She is steadfast in nothing except her unchanging fickleness.
We too have flourished as well, but the bloom of that flower was fleeting,
20   My fire flamed out of straw and was brief as the fuel it consumed.

So that, however, you may not fill your mind wholly with fierce joy
       I have not lost every hope of placating the wrath of that god,
Either because my error fell short of crime, though it is not
       Free from all shame, nonetheless my fault does not deserve hate,
25 Or because the wide world from the set of sun to its eastward rising,
       That world which obeys only him, has nothing more gentle than he.
Just as there is no force by which he can be overcome and
       Just so his heart becomes soft toward those who offer meek prayers,
And in the manner of gods, to whose company he'll ascend some day,
30   When he pardons my error he will grant me still other requests.
If you should count up the days of sunshine and cloud through the whole year
       You will find that the days when the sun is shining outnumber the rest.

And lest you delight overmuch at my ruin consider the fact that
       Some time in the future I may also be saved and restored;

136

35 Think that when Caesar is softened it is possible that you may see
    My face in the middle of Rome once more though you're sad at the sight
And that I may see you in turn exiled for more serious reason:
    This is the wish that I make only next to the first of my vows.

9

O if you would allow me to mention your name in my poems
    How often would you have been mentioned in them before!
I should write of you only, remembering your kindness; in my books
    Not one single page would be finished without some reference to you.
5 The debt that I owe you would be made known everywhere through the City.
    If, exiled as I am, I am read in the City I've lost.
The present would know you as gentle, the age that comes after would know it,
    If only my writings achieve some permanence in days to come.
The learned reader would not discontinue the song of your praises:
10   This is the honor you'd win because you have rescued your bard.

This is the first gift of Caesar, that I still breathe and am living,
    This is the thanks I must give to you after I've thanked the great gods.
Caesar has spared my life; you preserve the life he has given,
    And you bring it about that I may enjoy the gift I've received.
15 When the greatest share of my friends was horrified at my misfortune
    And some of them tried to pretend that they were afraid it would come
And looked down as if from a height on my ship as it foundered in shipwreck
    Nor extended a hand to the man who was swimming through terrible waves,
You were the only one who called me back half-dead from Styx river:

20   This too is your work, that I can remember your kindness to me.
          May the gods together with Caesar declare themselves friends to you always:
              None of my prayers then could be more comprehensive than this.

      All this my labor would place, if only you would allow me,
          In my brilliantly worded books to be seen in the brightest of lights.
25   Now too although she's been ordered to maintain her silence my Muse is
          Scarcely restrained from her wish to name you although you resist.
      As a hound that has come on the traces of a timorous deer while out hunting
          Is restrained by the unyielding leash as he struggles against it in vain,
      As the race horse beyond the barrier when the gates have not yet been flung open
30   Strives now with hoof, now with forehead to knock down the door which confines,
      So does my Muse, who is bound and gagged by the ban you've laid on her,
          Desire to speak for your glory the name she's forbidden to speak.

      Yet lest your feelings be hurt by the zeal of a duty-bound comrade
          I shall obey your command—do not be afraid I shall not.
35   But I should not be compliant if you did not think I'd remembered:
          That which you do not prevent by saying so—grateful I'll be.
      And while—may it be O so brief—I shall look on the light of my living
          This spirit of mine shall perform this duty of friendship toward you.

10

Since I've been here in the Pontus the Danube has frozen thrice over,
    The waves of the Euxine ocean have hardened as well three times.

138

And it seems now I've been far from my country just so long a time
As Dardanian Troy was besieged by the Grecian army—ten years.
5   So slowly the time goes you'd think it was standing still in its traces
And the year takes its way as though it were dragging its footsteps along.
The summer solstice deprives me of nothing at all from the nighttime
Nor does the winter solstice make shorter each of my days.

Can it be in my case that nature has taken unusual posture
10   And does she make everything long as the wearisome length of my cares?
Or does that time common to all pursue its accustomed progress
While the time that's peculiar to me is simply more harsh in my life,
I whom the shore of the Euxine, the sea that is falsely denoted,
Holds now and the left (and ill-omened) land of the Scythian strait?

15   The numberless races around me menace with terrible warfare,
These people who think it is shameful to live without plundering men;
Nothing beyond me lacks danger; the hill is defended around it
By the slightest of walls, the strategic position that favors the place.
Whenever you least expect it, like a bird the enemy gathered
20   In a dense mass flies past us and, scarce seen, drives its booty along.
Often inside of the walls when the gates have been shut quite securely,
We have picked up their poisoned arrows flung into the midst of the roads.
It's a rare farmer who dares to till his acres, and he with
One hand (poor devil) goes plowing, with the other he handles his sword.
25   Under his helmet the shepherd blows on straws joined with pitch-gum
And instead of a wolf the trembling sheep stand in dread of war.
We are scarcely defended within the fortress and even within it

139

The barbarous crowd mixed with Greeks still inspires our hearts with fear.
In fact, the barbarians live with us without discrimination
30   And they possess more than half of the houses which shelter us.
Even though you don't fear them you would hate them all when you see them,
          Their chests covered over with hides and their heads with long hanging hair.
And even those men who're believed to descend from Greek colonizers
          Wear Persian trousers instead of the garments their own nation wears.

35   They carry on their relations by means of their common language
          While I am reduced to communication by making signs.
Here I am the barbarian, and I'm understood by no one,
          And the stupid Getae make fun of the Latin words which I speak;
And openly often they speak ill of me and with perfect freedom,
40   Perhaps even holding against me the fact that I'm exiled from Rome.
And as it happens, they think I am crazy when to their jabber
          I nod my head to say "yes" and shake it to signify "no."
Add that an unjust justice is enforced with the rigid sword blade
          And wounds are frequently given in the midst of the market place.

45   O harsh Lachesis, who gave me, born under a star that's unlucky,
          The threads of a life that were not shorter than those which are mine!
The fact that I lack the sight of my fatherland and of my comrades
          And that I live here among the Scythian race I lament:
Both of these penalties are grave, but I deserved the loss of my City;
50   Perhaps I did not deserve to be punished in such a place.
Why do I speak? I'm a madman. I deserved to lose even my life then
          When I did injury to the power of Caesar the god.

11

That someone, I don't know who, has insulted you, called you the wife of
    An exile is the complaint your latest letter has brought.
I was sorry, not so much because my fate has a bad reputation,
    Something a wretch like me has accustomed his spirit to bear,
5   As because—the last thing I wished you—I've caused your humiliation
    And because I suppose you have blushed as you thought of my shame and my grief.
Endure and be steadfast; you've suffered much graver reverses than this is
    At the time when the anger of Caesar snatched me away from you.

This fellow's deceived, however, by whose judgment I'm called an exile:
10   A gentler penalty followed upon the mistake I made.
My greatest punishment is to have offended him and before I
    Did so I wish that the hour of my death had come upon me.
My boat, nonetheless, was shaken, not sunk or completely swallowed,
    And although as yet it has found no port it still floats on the waves.
15   Neither my life nor my wealth nor my citizen's right has he taken
    From me who deserved to lose all on account of my grievous fault.
But because no criminal act was joined to the sin I committed
    He did nothing more than forbid me to stay at my paternal hearth,
And just as he's acted toward others, whose numbers I cannot now count up,
20   The power of Caesar has been as mild as it's been toward me.
He uses the word "relegated" and not the name of "exile" for me:
    My case and my cause are secure on account of the judgment he made.
With justice therefore my poems, Caesar, as far as they're able
    And such as they are, they sing the highest praises of you.

25 With justice I pray to the gods that they close their threshold against you
    Thus far and desire that you should reign as a god without them:
The people voice the same wish; but as rivers flow into great ocean
    Just so is a trickle of water accustomed to flow there as well.

But you then by whom I am called an exile, cease to shout falsehoods,
30   Cease to weigh down my misfortune by naming it with an untruth.

12

You write and you bid me divert this tearful time with my verses
    So that my spirit won't break and rot in this miserable place.
It's hard, friend, to do what you ask since poetry's work for the happy
    Man and his poems require peace of mind for the task.
5 My fortunes are pummeled about by gales on an unfriendly ocean,
    There's nothing can possibly be any sadder than my sad lot.
You're asking that Priam go playing just after he's buried his children,
    And orphaned Niobe to lead off the dance at some festival game.
I think I'm restrained by my sorrows, and it seems I must be, from my verses,
10   Ordered to go as I am alone to the uttermost Getes.

Though you give me, a weakling, a heart that is bolstered up like an oak tree
    Such as the story relates the victim of Anytus had,
Wisdom will break and fall beneath such a weight of sheer ruin;
    The wrath of a god will prevail over a man's human strength.

15 That old man Socrates, called wise by Apollo, could not have
           In such a condition as mine written a single book.
   Although I should cease to recall my fatherland or remember you
           And every sense of the loss which I have sustained should depart
   Anxiety still would forbid me to exercise a poet's function,
20   Would forbid me to rest at my ease in a place ringed by unnumbered foes.

   Add also the fact that my talent, now eaten away with long rusting,
           Is languid and much less strong than it used to be once before.
   A fertile field when it is not renewed by its frequent plowing
           Will surely produce little else but thorns and some useless weeds.
25 The race horse who's stood a long while runs badly and when his contenders
           Are loosed at the race course barrier he will finish last every time.
   If a boat has been kept a long time away from the wharf and the water
           Where it is accustomed to be it gradually cracks and rots through.
   Give up your hope that I may, a little man as I was before,
30   Be able to equal that man such as I used to be.
   A long endurance of evils has crushed and worn down my talents
           And out of the vigor I had there isn't a particle left.

   If nonetheless, as even now, I took up my writing tablets
           And wished to compel my words into their regular feet
35 My poems would not come through or they'd be the sort that I send you,
           Worthy of their master's time, worthy of their master's place.

   Finally, glory gives no small impetus to a poet's
           Mind, and the love of praise causes that mind to create.
   Once I was drawn by the glitter that goes with a name and with glory

40   While a strong favoring breeze pushed my sail yards along.
        Now things are not so well with me that I should seek after glory:
           If I could bring it to pass, no one would know me at all.

        Or is it because at first my poems found success you persuade me
           To write and to follow up the earlier triumph I had?
45   Let it be said with all due respect to you, the nine sisters:
           You are the principal cause of the exile to which I was forced.
        And just as the man who created the brazen bull was punished justly
           So do I suffer with justice because of my *Arts of Love.*
        I should not have anything more to do with the writing of verses
50   As, having been shipwrecked, I should henceforth avoid every sea.

        But, I wonder, if I should resume in my madness that fatal endeavor
           Would this place provide me with the equipment for writing a poem?
        There isn't a book to be found, there's no one to read any poem to,
           Nor is there a person at hand who can understand what I may say.
55   The entire region is one of barbaric, animal voices,
           Everywhere filled with the sounds of fear and the clamor of war.
        I seem to myself to have lost the power to speak my own language
           For I have learned how to speak Sarmatian and Getic instead.

        And yet, to confess you the truth, I find that I am quite unable
60   To prevent my Muse from her task in the composition of verse.
        I've written books and when they were written consumed them in fire:
           The total result of my work is a little hot heap of ash.
        I am not able to write any verses and yet I desire
           To write them: and therefore my poems are consigned to the flames and destroyed.

65 Not unless some of them were perchance snatched away by deception
      Would any part of my toil and my talent have come to your hands.
Thus do I wish that my *Art*, which destroyed its creator, a man who
      Stood in no dread of that fate, had likewise been turned into ash!

13

This is the "Good Health" your Naso sends you from the region of Tomis,
      If anyone's able to send that which he lacks himself.
For the sickness of mind that I suffer has infected my body likewise
      So there's no part of me which is free from the torture that I undergo.
5 And day after day I am racked by the torments which grip my rib cage
      From the onslaught of intense freezing which the savage winter provides.
If nevertheless you are healthy then in some part as well I am healthy:
      For my ruin has found support from the shoulders you offered me.

Why, when you gave me your pledges in a most handsome manner,
      When on all counts you lent me protection of life and limb,
10 Why do you sin in sending so rarely a letter to cheer me
      And offer your sincere service but deny me your written words?
Do better than this, I pray you, because if you make this amendment
      There won't be a spot that will blemish that perfect body of yours.
15 I would make still more accusations if it weren't for the possible reason
      That although I receive no letter, nonetheless a letter was sent.
May the gods grant that there's no foundation for the complaint I'm making against you
      And that I'm mistaken when I think that you have forgotten me.
What I pray for is real, that's apparent; for me it's not right to believe that

20 The sturdy and steadfast devotion of your heart has been changed toward me.
    May the white-leaved wormwood be absent from the chilly shores of the Pontus
        And rather the sweet thyme of Hybla be missing from Sicily
  Than that anyone should bring me proof that you have forgotten a comrade:
        Not so black as this thought are the threads which the Fates have woven for me.
25 But you, nonetheless, to be able to refute this false charge that you're guilty
        Beware that you do not appear to be something which you are not.
  And as once we used to consume the long days of our friendship with talking
        When the time was too short for the many things which we had to say
  So may our letters convey to and fro the words which are silent
30   And our hands and papyrus perform the functions of language for us.
  In order that I should not seem to have too little faith that we're able
        To communicate thus (it's enough with these verses to give you advice)
  Receive the last word which a letter employs when it comes to its closing—
        May your fate be far from what mine is and here is that word: "Farewell."

14

How great a memorial I have erected for you in my writings,
    O wife who is dearer to me than myself, you can see for yourself.
Though fortune may take away much from the author of what are my poems
    You nonetheless shall reach fame because of my talents and art.
5 As long as my poems are read your name shall be read with my verses,
    You shall not completely be lost when you go to your sorrowful pyre.
And although you may rouse people's pity because of your husband's misfortune
    You will find some women who'd wish to be just the woman you are,
Who indeed because you're a part of and share in my dismal reverses

10 Will call you a blessed woman and envy your sorrowful state;
I could not have given you more than this if I'd given you riches:
        The ghost of the rich man will carry nothing with him to the grave.
I have given to you the enjoyment of a name which will be immortal
        And this, beyond which I could give nothing that's greater, you have.

15 Add also the fact that you are the sole protectress of my fortunes
        And to you there comes a no small part of that burden of pride,
That my voice has never been silent in singing your praises and that you
        Ought to be proud with the proofs your husband displays of your worth.
In order that no one may say that this praise was unwise, be persistent
20   And minister equally to both me and your love and your faith.

For your excellence, while I was unharmed, remained free from hint of reproaches
        And was uprightness only, untouched by any reason for blame.
Now there's a space that's been cleared for you by the crash of my fortunes;
        Here let your virtue erect a construction the whole world can see.
25 It's easy enough for a wife to be good when what hinders is absent
        And she finds no obstacle there to keep her from doing her part.
When the god thunders out in the heavens, not to shrink away from the stormcloud—
        That shows a wife's loyalty, that is the true married love.

Rare indeed is the virtue unswayed by the guidance of Fortune
30   Which abides with a posture that's firm when Fortune who tried it departs.
Yet when virtue herself is the prize and the goal of whatever's been sought for
        Even when fortunes are low she remains with her head held high.
Although you may count all of time no century will keep its silence
        About her, no place but admire wherever the world may extend.

147

35 Do you see how Penelope's faith in her husband throughout the long ages
    Has held its praises and her name is one that never dies?
Do you see how the wives of Admetus and Hector are sung by the poets,
    And the daughter of Iphis, who dared to ascend her husband's death-pyre?
How Laodamia still lives, whose husband was Protesilaus,
40   He who was first with his swift foot to touch upon Trojan soil?
I have no need for your death, I need only your love and your faith in
    Me; it is not difficult for you to find eternal fame.

And do not believe that I warn you because you're not doing your duty;
    I'm simply filling your sails although you're proceeding with oars.
45 Who gives you advice when you're doing your best merely praises your actions
    And by his exhortation approves everything that you've done.

NOTES

BOOK I

1

5. Vaccinium: the whortleberry, v. myrtillus Linnaeus.
7. Minium: red lead, used for coloring.
79. Phaethon drove the chariot of his father, the Sun, and destroyed himself; see Ovid, *Metamorphoses* 2, 1–328.
89. The story of Icarus is told by Ovid in *Metamorphoses* 8, 152–259.
99. Achilles had wounded Telephus and an oracle said only Achilles could heal him. This he did with the rust of the spear he had used to wound Telephus: Ovid, *Metamorphoses* 12, 112; 13, 171.
114. Both Oedipus and Telegonus killed their fathers.
117. The fifteen books of the *Metamorphoses*, on which Ovid was still working when he was exiled.

2

7. Turnus, king of the Rutulians, was Aeneas' great adversary in the *Aeneid*.
50. The tenth wave in a series was considered the most dangerous by the Romans.

5

21. The Phocian friend of Orestes was Pylades.

6

1. Antimachus came from Claros.
2. The poet of Cos was Philetas.
25. That princess is Livia, the wife of Augustus.

7

13. The *Metamorphoses* are meant here; Ovid says he destroyed them but obviously copies survived at Rome. The friend to whom this poem is addressed (as is III, 14) was probably Ovid's publisher or at least agent.
17. Althaia, the mother of Meleager, angered because he had killed her brother, burned the brand upon which her son's life depended.

9

32. Theseus tried to rescue his friend Pirithous from Hades.

10

2. Cassis is the word for helmet used here: hence the ship was named "Cassis," or "Helmet of Minerva."
26. Priapus was the god of Lampsacus.
27. Helle, for whom the Hellespont was named, is the hapless virgin.

11

15. Bootes is the guardian mentioned.

BOOK II

19. Telephus was the ruler of Teuthras; see notes at I, 1, 99 and v, 2, 15.
26. The Secular Games, celebrated in 17 B.C. by Augustus to honor Apollo and the new government at Rome.
94. Ovid had served on the board of the centumviri, a court for civil suits especially dealing with inheritances.
103–106. This passage has given rise to the con-

jecture that Ovid was banished because he saw Livia in her bath.
168. The "zodiac figures of youth" (*sidus iuvenale*) are the grandsons of Augustus. Drusus who was the son, and Germanicus, the adopted son, of Tiberius, are here described in flattering terms as a constellation.
190. The Great Bear constellation is meant by "the Parrhasian girl."
199–200. Tomis lay in the province of Moesia, which was first ruled by a Roman governor in A.D. 6; the region had very recently been added to the Roman empire.
225–230. Ovid reviews the wars of Augustus from 20 B.C. to A.D. 10; they include the return of the standards captured from Crassus at Carrhae in 53 B.C. to Augustus in 20 B.C., primarily a political victory.
229. The warrior offspring is Tiberius.
245–250. These lines are quoted with some deliberate inexactitude from *Art of Love* I, 31–34.
260. Ilia was the daughter of Aeneas, who by Mars became the mother of Romulus and Remus, according to Ennius' *Annales;* she is also known as Rhea Silvia in Livy.
261. *Aeneadum genetrix* are the first words of Lucretius, *De Rerum Natura.*
294. Erichthonius was the child of Pallas Athena and Hephaestus, born out of wedlock, in the earliest form of the myth.

297. Io, driven by Juno from Argos, because Jupiter loved her; her cow-form caused an identification of Io with the Egyptian cow-goddess Isis.

305. The reference here is to passing over consecrated ground, a *locus sacer*, which constituted sacrilege. If the taboo involved was broken the priest who had forbidden the violation was free from guilt. The priest suggests Ovid, who forbade Roman matrons from reading his *Art of Love;* the poet, moreover, is the priest of the Muses.

304. See note II, 245–250.

339. The juvenile poems of Ovid to which he refers here are the *Amores*, written in his early manhood; his "false love" (340) is Corinna, his possibly fictitious mistress, although his contemporaries firmly believed in her existence.

359–360. To judge a poet's character from his poems would lead to such absurdities as these, since Accius wrote about cruelties, Terence about parasites, and others about warfare.

386. Pelops, son of Tantalus, had an ivory shoulder replacing the one Demeter had chewed off when he was served as a meal to the gods in his infancy. He later went to Pisa in Elis, where his famous chariot race with Oenomaus won him the hand of Hippodamia.

387. The mother is Medea, who killed her children by Jason.

389–390. The story of Philomela, Tereus, Procne, and Itys is referred to here; it is told by Ovid, *Metamorphoses* 6. 412–674.

391. Thyestes, brother of Atreus, seduced the latter's wife, Aerope. Atreus, in revenge, killed the sons of Thyestes and served them to him as a meal. The sun turned away in horror and set in the east on the day of the banquet, as is told by the scholiast to Euripides, *Orestes* 812.

397. Bellerophon of Corinth killed the monster Chimaera and was almost destroyed by the machinations of Antea (or Stheneboea) and her husband Proetus, king of Tiryns, because Bellerophon rejected Antea's advances.

400. Cassandra, priestess of Phoebus Apollo, was taken home to Mycenae by Agamemnon after the Trojan War, where she was murdered by Clytaemnestra.

401. Danae's daughter-in-law was Andromeda, whom Perseus saved from a sea-monster. The mother of Lyaeus (Bacchus) was Semele of Thebes; his father was Zeus.

402. Haemon was Antigone's lover. The night was lengthened into two for Alcmena, wife of Amphitryon, when she was visited by Zeus, who begot Hercules with her.

403. The son-in-law of Pelias was Admetus of Pherae, the husband of Alcestis; Theseus carried off Ariadne from Crete and deserted her in

Naxos; Protesilaus was the first Greek fighter to set foot on Trojan soil in the Trojan War.

405. Deianira, wife of Hercules, killed Iole when she discovered Hercules loved her.

406. Hylas and Ganymede were handsome boys; the first was loved by Hercules, the second by Zeus.

409. The satyric drama is meant here, a kind of comic play usually added to a dramatic trilogy.

415. Eubius may have written tales involving abortion. O. Immisch believed he wrote a medical poem as a hoax.

417. Sybaris, known for the loose behavior of its citizens, produced salacious stories in verse, especially those by Hemitheon.

418. Such writers were Astyanassa, Elephantis, and Philaenis, all Greek female authors of obscene works.

425. Sea, land, and sky formed the three-fold universe of Lucretius v, 93–94.

437. Evidently Perilla, the Roman poetess, wrote under this assumed name until the death of her husband Metellus allowed her to write under his name.

439. P. Terentius Varro Atacinus wrote an epic called *Argonautica*, based on the work of Apollonius Rhodius, describing the voyage of the Argonauts to Colchis, whose chief river is the Phasis.

464. Augustus became known as Augustus in 27 B.C.

487. Ovid himself wrote a manual on cosmetics *De Medicamine Faciei*. The handbooks on games, sports, and crafts he mentions show what a large role was assigned to didactic poetry in Roman literature.

519. These were probably some of the *Heroides* of Ovid.

525–527. The Telamonian Ajax and Medea were the subjects of pictures by Timomachus of Byzantium, the last of the great Greek painters; he is said to have been very skillful in the portrayal of conflicting emotions. Venus rising from the sea was painted by Apelles, in the 4th century B.C.

549. The *Fasti* described the religious festivals of Rome according to the calendar; Ovid may have blocked out and partly written the books for the last six months of the year but only the *Fasti* for the first six months survive.

553. Ovid wrote a tragedy called *Medea* but only two lines of it survive; it was probably intended for recitation rather than presentation on the stage.

556–557. The *Metamorphoses*.

1

36. The oaken crown was given to Augustus as the savior of the Roman people, but the oak tree was also sacred to Jupiter.

42. Apollo is the god of Leucas and his temple stood near Actium, where Augustus won the great naval victory against Antony and Cleopatra in 31 B.C. The palace of Augustus was by senate decree adorned with oak and laurel boughs.

62-72. The statues of Danaus, grandson of Belus, and his daughters stood in the portico of the temple of Apollo on the Palatine, where a library had been set up by Augustus; another was located in the portico of Octavia near the theater of Marcellus, also established by Augustus. Asinius Pollio had founded a library in the temple of Liberty. Ovid's poems were evidently banned from all these public libraries.

2

2. Callisto, daughter of Lycaon, was also known as Arctos, the constellation of the Bear.

3. The Pierian sisters are the Muses, and the offspring of Leto is Apollo, the protector and sponsor of the Muses.

3

62. The Samian sage is Pythagoras of Samos, whose views on the transmigration of souls were well known.

67. Antigone of Thebes buried her brother, Polynices.

4

27. Eumedes' son was Dolon, who tried to steal the horses of Achilles at Troy.

29-30. The myth of Phaethon is told by Ovid, *Metamorphoses* 2, 1-343.

5

18. His friend's name might have been Carus, "dear."

39. The Emathian leader is Alexander the Great, who showed clemency to his Persian enemies, Porus and Darius.

42. Hercules married Hebe, daughter of Juno.

7

42. Irus was the beggar who lived in the house of Ulysses at Ithaca; Croesus was the fabulously rich king of Lydia.

8

1. Triptolemus was the son of Celeus, king of Eleusis, and known as the inventor of agriculture and later as a judge in Hades.

9

6. The story of Medea and her flight from Colchis is the sole etiological myth in the *Tristia*.
34. Ovid evidently derives the name Tomis from the Greek verb *temno*, I cut.

10

73. Acontius loved Cydippe, as told in Ovid's *Heroides* 20 and 21. He threw her an apple inscribed with the words, "I swear by the sanctuary of Diana to marry Acontius," which she read aloud and then threw away. But by this act she was tricked into marrying Acontius, which might serve as a warning against the picking up of random apples.

11

28. The Thessalian steeds were the horses of Achilles, who dragged Hector's body up and down in front of the walls of Troy; see the last books of the *Iliad*.

39. Busiris was a king of Egypt who sacrificed strangers to Jupiter.

BOOK IV

2

1. Germany was the site of campaigning by Tiberius in A.D. 11; his triumph was celebrated on Jan. 16, A.D. 12.

3

1. The Great and Small Bear, constellations in the sky.
77. Tiphys was the pilot of the Argo, in which the Argonauts sailed to Colchis in southern Russia.

4

19. The two gods are Jupiter and Augustus.
67. The Pelopian maiden is Iphigenia, who, in one version of her sacrifice by her father Agamemnon, was rescued by Diana to become her priestess in the Tauric Chersonese and a deer was substituted for her at Aulis.
71. See note 1, 5, 21.

10

6. In 43 B.C. the consuls Hirtius and Pansa defeated Antony in battle at Mutina and died there; Ovid's birth was on March 20, 43 B.C.

13. The festival of Quinquatrus was March 19–23; on the final four days armed combats took place at Rome.
35. Ovid retained the narrower toga-stripe of the equestrian order instead of moving up to the senatorial order.
95. The Olympic games were celebrated every four years; four times ten makes Ovid forty, but these Olympiads are five years each, making him fifty years old when he was exiled.

BOOK V

2

15. See note 1, 1, 99.
76. Criminals were thrown from a cliff near the temple of Apollo on the promontory of Leucas.

3

26. Bacchus was born of Semele prematurely by means of a lightning stroke and again later from the thigh of Jupiter.
30. Capaneus is referred to here.
39–40. Lycurgus and Pentheus opposed the worship of Bacchus and were punished by him.
42. Ariadne was the wife of Bacchus.

5

38. The son of Battus was Callimachus, the Greek poet, who may have written on the subject of

the brothers Eteocles and Polynices of Thebes; they died at each other's hands.
53. Echion's fortress is Thebes in Boeotia.
54. Evadne was the wife of Capaneus, killed at Thebes; she leaped into his funeral pyre and died with him.
55. Alcestis was the most famous daughter of Pelias. Her husband was Admetus.
58. Laodamia's husband, Protesilaus, was the first Greek to set foot on Trojan soil.

6

7. Palinurus was the helmsman of Aeneas as he and the Trojans sailed for Italy.
9. Automedon was the driver of Achilles' chariot.
11. Podalirius was one of two physicians with the Greek army at Troy.
26. Orestes behaved strangely in the madness brought on him by the Furies.

7b

25. Parts of the *Heroides* may have been set to music and acted out on a stage.

10

45. Lachesis is that one of the three Fates who allots the thread of life.

12

12. The victim of Anytus was Socrates; see Plato's *Apology*.

14

38. The daughter of Iphis was Evadne. See note v, 5, 54.

BIBLIOGRAPHICAL NOTE

In addition to the two chief books on Ovid by Hermann Fraenkel, *Ovid: a Poet Between Two Worlds* (1945) and L. P. Wilkinson, *Ovid Recalled* (1955), the following articles are useful for an understanding of the theme, structure, and imagery of the *Tristia*:

R. J. Dickinson, "The 'Tristia': Poetry in Exile." In *Ovid*, ed. J. W. Binns. Greek and Latin Studies —Classical Literature and Its Influence. Routledge and Kegan Paul: London and Boston, 1973.

E. J. Kenney, "The Poetry of Ovid's Exile." *Proceedings of the Cambridge Philological Society*, N. S., 11 (1965): 37–49.

A. G. Lee, "An Appreciation of Tristia III. viii." *Greece and Rome*, 18 (1949): 113–120.

INDEX OF NAMES

157

NOTES

BOOK I

1

5. Vaccinium: the whortleberry, v. myrtillus Linnaeus.
7. Minium: red lead, used for coloring.
79. Phaethon drove the chariot of his father, the Sun, and destroyed himself; see Ovid, *Metamorphoses* 2, 1-328.
89. The story of Icarus is told by Ovid in *Metamorphoses* 8, 152-259.
99. Achilles had wounded Telephus and an oracle said only Achilles could heal him. This he did with the rust of the spear he had used to wound Telephus: Ovid, *Metamorphoses* 12, 112; 13, 171.
114. Both Oedipus and Telegonus killed their fathers.
117. The fifteen books of the *Metamorphoses*, on which Ovid was still working when he was exiled.

2

7. Turnus, king of the Rutulians, was Aeneas' great adversary in the *Aeneid*.
50. The tenth wave in a series was considered the most dangerous by the Romans.

5

21. The Phocian friend of Orestes was Pylades.

6

1. Antimachus came from Claros.
2. The poet of Cos was Philetas.
25. That princess is Livia, the wife of Augustus.

7

13. The *Metamorphoses* are meant here; Ovid says he destroyed them but obviously copies survived at Rome. The friend to whom this poem is addressed (as is III, 14) was probably Ovid's publisher or at least agent.
17. Althaia, the mother of Meleager, angered because he had killed her brother, burned the brand upon which her son's life depended.

9

32. Theseus tried to rescue his friend Pirithous from Hades.

10

2. Cassis is the word for helmet used here: hence the ship was named "Cassis," or "Helmet of Minerva."
26. Priapus was the god of Lampsacus.
27. Helle, for whom the Hellespont was named, is the hapless virgin.

11

15. Bootes is the guardian mentioned.

BOOK II

19. Telephus was the ruler of Teuthras; see notes at I, 1, 99 and v, 2, 15.
26. The Secular Games, celebrated in 17 B.C. by Augustus to honor Apollo and the new government at Rome.
94. Ovid had served on the board of the centumviri, a court for civil suits especially dealing with inheritances.
103–106. This passage has given rise to the conjecture that Ovid was banished because he saw Livia in her bath.
168. The "zodiac figures of youth" (*sidus iuvenale*) are the grandsons of Augustus. Drusus who was the son, and Germanicus, the adopted son, of Tiberius, are here described in flattering terms as a constellation.
190. The Great Bear constellation is meant by "the Parrhasian girl."
199–200. Tomis lay in the province of Moesia, which was first ruled by a Roman governor in A.D. 6; the region had very recently been added to the Roman empire.
225–230. Ovid reviews the wars of Augustus from 20 B.C. to A.D. 10; they include the return of the standards captured from Crassus at Carrhae in 53 B.C. to Augustus in 20 B.C., primarily a political victory.
229. The warrior offspring is Tiberius.
245–250. These lines are quoted with some deliberate inexactitude from *Art of Love* I, 31–34.
260. Ilia was the daughter of Aeneas, who by Mars became the mother of Romulus and Remus, according to Ennius' *Annales;* she is also known as Rhea Silvia in Livy.
261. *Aeneadum genetrix* are the first words of Lucretius, *De Rerum Natura.*
294. Erichthonius was the child of Pallas Athena and Hephaestus, born out of wedlock, in the earliest form of the myth.

297. Io, driven by Juno from Argos, because Jupiter loved her; her cow-form caused an identification of Io with the Egyptian cow-goddess Isis.

305. The reference here is to passing over consecrated ground, a *locus sacer*, which constituted sacrilege. If the taboo involved was broken the priest who had forbidden the violation was free from guilt. The priest suggests Ovid, who forbade Roman matrons from reading his *Art of Love;* the poet, moreover, is the priest of the Muses.

304. See note II, 245–250.

339. The juvenile poems of Ovid to which he refers here are the *Amores,* written in his early manhood; his "false love" (340) is Corinna, his possibly fictitious mistress, although his contemporaries firmly believed in her existence.

359–360. To judge a poet's character from his poems would lead to such absurdities as these, since Accius wrote about cruelties, Terence about parasites, and others about warfare.

386. Pelops, son of Tantalus, had an ivory shoulder replacing the one Demeter had chewed off when he was served as a meal to the gods in his infancy. He later went to Pisa in Elis, where his famous chariot race with Oenomaus won him the hand of Hippodamia.

387. The mother is Medea, who killed her children by Jason.

389–390. The story of Philomela, Tereus, Procne,

and Itys is referred to here; it is told by Ovid, *Metamorphoses* 6. 412–674.

391. Thyestes, brother of Atreus, seduced the latter's wife, Aerope. Atreus, in revenge, killed the sons of Thyestes and served them to him as a meal. The sun turned away in horror and set in the east on the day of the banquet, as is told by the scholiast to Euripides, *Orestes* 812.

397. Bellerophon of Corinth killed the monster Chimaera and was almost destroyed by the machinations of Antea (or Stheneboea) and her husband Proetus, king of Tiryns, because Bellerophon rejected Antea's advances.

400. Cassandra, priestess of Phoebus Apollo, was taken home to Mycenae by Agamemnon after the Trojan War, where she was murdered by Clytaemnestra.

401. Danae's daughter-in-law was Andromeda, whom Perseus saved from a sea-monster. The mother of Lyaeus (Bacchus) was Semele of Thebes; his father was Zeus.

402. Haemon was Antigone's lover. The night was lengthened into two for Alcmena, wife of Amphitryon, when she was visited by Zeus, who begot Hercules with her.

403. The son-in-law of Pelias was Admetus of Pherae, the husband of Alcestis; Theseus carried off Ariadne from Crete and deserted her in

Naxos; Protesilaus was the first Greek fighter to set foot on Trojan soil in the Trojan War.

405. Deianira, wife of Hercules, killed Iole when she discovered Hercules loved her.

406. Hylas and Ganymede were handsome boys; the first was loved by Hercules, the second by Zeus.

409. The satyric drama is meant here, a kind of comic play usually added to a dramatic trilogy.

415. Eubius may have written tales involving abortion. O. Immisch believed he wrote a medical poem as a hoax.

417. Sybaris, known for the loose behavior of its citizens, produced salacious stories in verse, especially those by Hemitheon.

418. Such writers were Astyanassa, Elephantis, and Philaenis, all Greek female authors of obscene works.

425. Sea, land, and sky formed the three-fold universe of Lucretius v, 93–94.

437. Evidently Perilla, the Roman poetess, wrote under this assumed name until the death of her husband Metellus allowed her to write under his name.

439. P. Terentius Varro Atacinus wrote an epic called *Argonautica*, based on the work of Apollonius Rhodius, describing the voyage of the Argonauts to Colchis, whose chief river is the Phasis.

64. Augustus became known as Augustus in 27 B.C.

7. Ovid himself wrote a manual on cosmetics *De Medicamine Faciei*. The handbooks on games, sports, and crafts he mentions show what a large role was assigned to didactic poetry in Roman literature.

519. These were probably some of the *Heroides* of Ovid.

525–527. The Telamonian Ajax and Medea were the subjects of pictures by Timomachus of Byzantium, the last of the great Greek painters; he is said to have been very skillful in the portrayal of conflicting emotions. Venus rising from the sea was painted by Apelles, in the 4th century B.C.

549. The *Fasti* described the religious festivals of Rome according to the calendar; Ovid may have blocked out and partly written the books for the last six months of the year but only the *Fasti* for the first six months survive.

553. Ovid wrote a tragedy called *Medea* but only two lines of it survive; it was probably intended for recitation rather than presentation on the stage.

556–557. The *Metamorphoses*.